"Concevitch does an excellent job of drawing parallels between sales execution and leading a business. Like a CEO, the salesperson is responsible for situational analysis, identifying patterns and opportunities that can impact the landscape, setting strategy, establishing a shared mission, gaining personal and collective commitment, and ensuring optimal execution across multiple constituents. His emphasis on perpetual learning and adjustment is a good lesson for any leader–and a key ingredient for every successful salesperson."

—David Gould, Chairman & CEO, Witness Systems, Inc.

"In a 'flatter' world, selling changes! The successful salesperson needs to be an extreme learner every day. Counter-Intuitive Selling provides a practical guide to the changing field of sales."

—Elliott Masie, CEO, The MASIE Center's Learning CONSORTIUM

"Counter-Intuitive Selling comes directly from Bill's proven track record as a very successful executive. Every single piece of advice in this great book is directly derived from real-world success stories and achievements, many of which I have witnessed over many years of acquaintance with 'BBC.' A great summary of wisdom and experience that cannot be found in conventional books on sales and marketing."

—Axel Leblois, Founder, the Wireless Internet Institute
Senior Fellow, United Nations Institute for Training and Research

"In a lively and enjoyable style, Counter-Intuitive Selling explains how to get the best value out of a sympathetic mentor, and how important it is continuously to challenge received wisdom. All the book's messages must be commended to all who want to succeed in persuading. Besides, it's a very good read."

—Sir Michael Bett CBE MA, former Deputy Chairman, BRITISH TELECOM

"Bill Byron Concevitch has done an incredible job of forcing us to re-examine tactical sales fundamentals in an effort to reach outside our comfort zone. This book provides succinct ideas that will enable the sales professional to break habitual routines and become more creative. These new techniques are provided in an easy to adopt step-by-step roadmap to higher performance."

—George F. Norton III, Senior Partner, Heidrick & Struggles

"Counter-Intuitive Selling is packed with proven tips and strategies for dealing with buyers in unexpected ways. Bill's creative acronyms, N.E.R.D., H.E.R.B., H.A.N.K, and G.U.I.D.O., probably will become standard terminology for many sales organizations, as will this book become standard reading for the most successful sales professionals."

—Bob Kantin, President of SalesProposals.com, co-author of Why Johnny Can't Sell . . . and What to Do About It

counter-intuitive selling
(koun´tər-ĭn-tōō´ ĭ-tĭv sel´ĭng)

n. Mastering
the art of the
unexpected.

BILL BYRON CONCEVITCH

 PUBLISHING

Vice President and Publisher: Maureen McMahon
Editorial Director: Jennifer Farthing
Acquisitions Editor: Karen Murphy
Production Editor: Mike Hankes
Production Artist: Janet Schroeder
Cover Designer: Gail Chandler

Published by Kaplan Publishing,
a division of Kaplan, Inc.

Printed in the United States of America

07 08 09   10 9 8 7 6 5 4 3 2 1

Kaplan Publishing books are available at special quantity discounts to use for sales promotions, employee premiums, or educational purposes. Please call our Special Sales Department to order or for more information at 800-621-9621, ext. 4444, e-mail kaplanpubsales@kaplan.com, or write to Kaplan Publishing, 30 South Wacker Drive, Suite 2500, Chicago, IL 60606-7481.

THIS BOOK IS DEDICATED TO:

Winnie, Carly, and Brandon.
They inspired me,
Improved my work,
And made me laugh when I needed it.

And to the other boys,
Billy, Andrew, and Ian.
When they were around they asked
*"What **are** you writing?"*

Especially to My Princess,
*Who is **always** there–*
First my soulmate, then my proofreader.

And to the Lord, who we thank every day.

Contents

Find Out "Who's Who" with the Decision-Maker Rater

PART THREE

Dialog That Sets You Apart—Even from Your "Old" Self

Conversations That You Have Never Had Until Now

When Building a Relationship Is Best Done from a Distance

Acknowledgments

The reason that mentors come alive within this book is because mentors are a critical component and lynchpin to success in the business world, and in the world of counter-intuitive selling.

The mentor within counter-intuitive selling is real. "Frank" is a composite of the four most influential mentors in my life: Bill Coles, Frank Cella, Sam Iorio, and J. Anthony (Tony) Donaldson.

Thank you, gentlemen, for shaping my spirit, my soul, and my career. You have been tough when I needed you to be, and encouraging when the odds were against me. Most importantly, you believed in me—*no matter what.*

I owe each of you an eternal debt of gratitude.

FOREWORD

In sales, you can get the lessons of experience in one of two ways: You can either learn by losing, which is very expensive, or you can read a book like this and learn from the experience of others. What is intuitive to a veteran salesperson is often counter-intuitive to a newer salesperson.

This book contains a treasury of lessons, techniques, and anecdotes which will benefit salespeople of any experience level. Unfortunately, most salespeople have to learn these lessons the hard way.

The challenge, however, is not just to read, become aware of, or even practice these techniques occasionally. Rather, it's to make them habits. Competitive advantage doesn't come from awareness alone. *Counter-Intuitive Selling* focuses on making these sales techniques and lessons habits that are executed consistently.

Today, buyers want different things from their salespeople than in years before. They want salespeople who can solve business problems with their solutions. Salespeople today need to handle the politics of the customer's organization to win and then drive change management to produce results and repeat business.

The lessons and anecdotes in this book are easy to read and apply because they are based on sales experiences— and they will help you not only survive, but thrive in today's new sales world.

Rick Page
Author of the International Bestsellers
Hope Is Not a Strategy: The 6 Keys to
Winning the Complex Sale

Make Winning a Habit: 20 Best Practices of
the World's Greatest Sales Forces

INTRODUCTION

Success in sales can be elusive. At other times when success is achieved, it's hard for other sales professionals to duplicate. Getting out of the numbers game and to a point where selling is rewarding, intriguing, **and fun** is the end game.

More than 25 years of practicing in the field of sales finally led to the development of counter-intuitive selling. Achieving success at several organizations—even when others told us that success was not possible—led to the refining and documenting of exactly what we did to accomplish that achievement.

Then, it hit me. All of the things we were doing to build business were working because *we were doing the opposite of what our clients expected from us.* And more importantly, *we were doing the opposite of what all of the other sales professionals were doing!* We were standing out from the pack, building an impressive stable of blue chip, highly desirable clients, and landing the business, in spite of the odds.

It was all working as a result of doing the opposite of what we were conditioned to do as seasoned sales professionals! Was it hard to change our old ways and habits?

Absolutely!

Was it paying off when we continually refined our new ways and did the opposite of what we would have done in the past?

Absolutely!

Can you apply all of this to significantly change your results and lead the pack as you enter the world of counter-intuitive selling?

Absolutely!

This is where the adventure and journey begin . . .

part one

Changing Your Mindset
(and Habits)
Will Change Your Results

Counter-Intuitive Selling Requires a Mind Open to Change

Entering the world of counter-intuitive selling starts with a plan

chapter one

Why Counter-Intuitive Selling Is Harder Than It Sounds

What sounds logical—even easy—is actually one of the hardest things you will ever do. That's why this book is written quite differently from other sales books. Follow the plan outlined here, and your sales career will change—forever.

We were about to begin our weekly sales meeting. The most interesting and valuable part of any of our meetings is the time we spend sharing our successes and challenges from the week—real lessons learned, both good and bad. These lessons offer unique opportunities to learn from each other and to continue to change our behavior in order to achieve different results.

As we started, I shared the agenda, mentioning that the lessons we'd learned from our successes and challenges would be discussed during the wrap-up. As I always do at this point, I turned to the team and asked them to let me know what else we needed to add to the list of topics to cover.

Phil immediately spoke first. "Nothing to add," he began. "It all sounds good. I would like to suggest we start with the lessons learned, especially from Ken. We've all heard that he made some progress with Zucor this past week. We're curious as to how he got the meeting and how he got the agreement to use our solution in a major project. I admit that I'm curious from a selfish standpoint; I was the last one to try and work that account, and I could *not* get it to move."

The rest of the team agreed with Phil, so we decided to rearrange our agenda and start with a recap of the progress Ken was making with Zucor. Zucor was a high-potential prospect of ours (having all of the characteristics that could drive seven-figure yearly revenue for us) that several members of the team had worked—*and* worked, *and* worked, *and* worked. Over the past 18 months, we had achieved a net result of "zero revenue/zero progress."

Phil was the most recent team member to attempt to deliver with Zucor. About three months earlier, he had suggested to the team that he turn the account over to someone else. The team unanimously agreed and the account was turned over to Ken.

Since then, Ken updated the team on his progress (or lack of progress) with Zucor during our weekly meetings. The word circulated during the past week that Ken had broken through and that we had landed a major piece of business inside Zucor, with the potential for another large deal within the next six months. Now the team was interested to hear what Ken had accomplished, how he had accomplished it, and what we could all learn from the turn of events.

What Ken shared with the team in our meeting that day was just one of the dozens of real-life success stories that you will experience first-hand as you continue to read *Counter-Intuitive Selling: Mastering the Art of the Unexpected*. Ken's success story is not what is most important at this moment. You will have plenty of time to absorb it later, where it is highlighted in Chapter 18. What is important here is that you recognize the process and practice out of which counter-intuitive selling was born.

Leading by Example Is the Ultimate Mentoring Tool

A long-standing practice that I have with any sales team I lead is to never take any accounts from which team members can potentially earn a living. However, I unequivocally believe that **any sales leader must continually sell and produce**. Every sales leader (some call themselves sales managers) must maintain some accounts (prospects and customers) that are truly their own to lead over the finish line. Without demonstrating that you can master the sales relationship, the sales process, and everything that goes with it, how do you ever earn the respect of the teams that you lead?

By now you are probably thinking to yourself, "I'm just a few pages into this book and this guy is already confusing me! How can you have accounts of your own as a sales manager and yet not take any accounts away from your team?"

I admit that there is one small piece of the equation that I have failed to share. I never work any account—whether it is an existing customer or a prospect—**unless the team asks me to do it**.

So, you ask, why would they want me to work an account? Why would they give it up (along with the commission that will come with any sale from this account)? It is only when they have **nothing more to lose and everything to gain**.

First of all, it is not just one person that gives up the account—it is the team as a whole, unanimously. Each and every member of the sales team needs to say about the account, "We give up! We've tried everything. We have attempted every possible strategy and every technique we know to get business from this customer or prospect, and we've run out of things to try. We can't get there (get the customer over the finish line for the sale) from here, so you take it."

Then, and only then, does the prospect become mine. At the same time it becomes a teaching and learning experience for the team as a whole. These "impossible" accounts now become a live practice field on which I can demonstrate and prove to the team the power of counter-intuitive selling, reporting back to the team on my progress during our weekly meetings. Zucor was one of those accounts. I had taken over the Zucor account for about six months. Just recently, I had reassigned it to Ken as a reward for his efforts on some other challenging accounts.

This approach to sales management is the format and venue under which I have found it most effective to teach what this book is about: the art of counter-intuitive selling. Dealing with these most challenging accounts requires a different level of thinking—and it requires the ability to think and act differently.

Finding Success Through Change

People define insanity in many different ways, but one of the mentors in my life shared with me what I consider to be the best definition of the term: **insanity is doing the same things we've always done and expecting different results**. If this is true, then we need to change what we are doing, and begin to practice "things" that will change our results for the better.

We've all heard that "practice makes perfect." This is the farthest thing from the truth that has ever been stated. In reality, **practice makes permanent**. When you consider that practice is all about repetition, you begin to see why it often is not the formula for success if the wrong things are being repeated. I have met many unsuccessful salespeople who claim that they practice and prepare. But how can you know whether you are practicing the right things in the right way?

Everything you read in this book is born out of learning and mastering the art of counter-intuitive selling and leveraging the power of the unexpected. Everything is real; the successes of this process have all been repeated again and again. It works, and it can work for you— *but only if you follow the process and practices shared in the first six chapters of this book.*

A little later in the book, you will read a lot more about something that is the key to success when tackling new ways to do things (new behaviors). The technique is called "**time-spaced repetition**," and it is what practicing the right way is all about. For now, just tuck away in the back of your mind that using weekly sales meetings as the perfect vehicle for time-spaced repetition is a key to success.

Most salespeople will find ideas, concepts, and practices in this book that are radically different from their current sales techniques. As much as you may try, you will find it difficult to make changes in the way you sell, even though you believe you must change in order to improve your results. This is why the plan this book provides is just as important as any individual ideas or selling techniques contained between its covers.

If you are reading this book as a sales manager or sales leader, leading and managing a team of sales producers and sales reps, then I encourage you to consider adopting this format and process of teaching counter-intuitive selling to your team. If you are a sales producer or sales rep reading this book, then I encourage you to immediately share this book with your sales manager and ask him or her to consider adopting this style and format as a means of helping you and your team to master the art of counter-intuitive selling.

Before you begin reading Chapter 2, take your first step toward being successful in your journey into the world of counter-intuitive selling. **Start by stopping.** Stop for a minute to practice the first set of **The Successful Seven: Action Steps for Mastering the Art of Counter-Intuitive Selling**.

Change is up to you; so get started now!

The Successful Seven: Chapter 1

Action Steps for Mastering the Art of Counter-Intuitive Selling

1. Commit to changing the results of your sales career by following the plan in this book.

2. Personally commit to yourself that as you read this book, **you will not start a new chapter until you complete The Successful Seven** at the end of the current chapter.

3. Realize that the only way to significantly change your current results is by significantly changing your current behavior and mindset.

4. Understand that learning your current selling habits took a long time (perhaps longer than you think), so **changing your habits will take time and effort**.

5. If you are a salesperson (individual contributor), suggest to your sales manager that your team incorporate the "lessons learned" format into your weekly sales meetings.

6. If you are a sales leader (you manage and lead a group of sales professionals), immediately begin to incorporate the "lessons learned" format into your weekly sales meetings.

7. Realize that the **journey through counter-intuitive selling requires repetition on a regular basis** in order to be successful in changing your current results—and commit to following the **repetitive practice** plans in this book.

chapter two

Habits:
Our Best Friends and
Worst Enemies

This chapter has nothing to do with your selling career, and at the same time, everything to do with the future success of your selling career. So if success through change is what you are after, read this chapter carefully.

Simply defined, our habits are automatic behaviors—what we do without thinking. The good news is that habits, once formed, become natural. The bad news is that bad habits are hard to break.

If you think that habits are no big deal, and that habits are easy to change, then try this little exercise:

Fold your arms in front of you the way you always do—simply put one arm over the other. How does it feel? You will probably say that it feels natural or normal.

Now, unfold your arms. Fold them again, except this time, fold them in the opposite way—take the arm you had on top before and put it on the bottom. How does this feel? Perhaps a little strange. Tell yourself that from now on, whenever you fold your arms, you are going to fold your arms in the "new" way.

Got it? Great.

I bet the next time you find yourself with your arms folded, you will have folded them the "old" way, even though you made a conscious decision not to. Doing things the "old" way is a hard habit to break. But there is a way.

Every time I speak to a room full of sales professionals, some-where along the way in the presentation I slip in that exercise. I always get a big kick out of watching a large group of ego-driven, high-per-forming salespeople try to convince themselves that they can easily change the way they fold their arms. They usually place bets between each other (which I entice them to do!) and high-five each other with their contagious enthusiasm. Then something amusing happens: they fail miserably when they try to carry out their mission!

It Takes More Than a Decision to Change Your Actions

There is a very simple explanation as to why we cannot change the way we fold our arms by simply making the decision. **Conscious decisions alone do not change behavior.**

Why? Our behavior is driven by habits, and **habits are formed over time**—usually a long period of time.

Think about the arm-folding exercise. How long have you been folding your arms? My daughter Carly, who is now 3 years old, has al-ready been folding her arms for at least a year. By the time she is 20, she will have 18 years of practicing the way she folds her arms.

Even at 3 years old, she no longer has to think about how she will fold her arms—she just does it by habit. Do you think she will have much success at changing the way she folds her arms, even if she makes a conscious decision that she wants to change? Twenty years from now, after 23 years of forming and reinforcing the habit of fold-ing her arms in a specific way, how successful do you think she might be at changing her habit—her way?

I would even venture to say that if one day Carly wakes up and finds that, for some reason, it is suddenly a little painful to fold her arms the way she normally folds them, that she will still fold them the same way and endure the pain.

However, there is good news in this story, and it can have dramatic impact on your success in your selling career.

If Carly decides that she wants to (or needs to, as the case may be in your selling career) forever change the way she folds her arms, she needs to set time aside to practice the new way to fold her arms as soon as she has made the decision to change.

Now here's the trick. Carly needs to take the time to practice this new way—her new habit—for at least 21 consecutive days. Research shows that it takes at least 21 days of doing something new the same way, day in and day out without fail, in order to break an old habit and form a new one.

How many times have you said to yourself that you were going to treat your next sales call differently—not falling into the same old trap that you always do? And how many times, when it came to that critical moment in the phone call or face-to-face meeting when you needed to act differently in order to get the desired result, did you actually do something different? How many times have you said to yourself that you are not going to do or say the same old thing again, only to find that you go right ahead and do or say the same old thing again?

Building a New Comfort Zone Through Practice

In the next chapter, we'll discuss the role that your comfort zone plays in your habits. For now, just realize that trying something new, even when you know it will produce a better outcome, does not always feel comfortable. This fear of the unknown also adds to the challenge of moving to a new and different habit. It will not feel comfortable at first.

You Can't Afford to Have to Think

My father was a sports writer for a major portion of his career. He had the opportunity to meet some of the real stars of his day and also to learn from their successes, their failures, and their habits. One day, he shared with me the story of one of his colleagues, Jack, who was doing a story on Ozzie Smith, one of the best infielders ever to play baseball.

The writer decided that before he would take Ozzie's valuable time for an interview, he would follow Ozzie over the course of about 25 games. He wanted to see if Ozzie had a routine that he followed as he prepared to play each game.

As the writer followed Ozzie from ballpark to ballpark, he noticed something that struck him as quite puzzling. When the time finally came for the face-to-face interview, Jack could not wait to ask Ozzie about what he had been observing.

The time came to pose the question, so Jack began: "Ozzie, before we begin the formal interview, I would just like to ask you a simple question. I've now followed you for about 25 games, from ballpark to ballpark, and I think I've picked up on something. Before every game, you arrive a few hours before any other player, and you shag (catch) about 200 to 300 ground balls from one of the coaches. After that, when the rest of the team arrives at the ballpark, you go through all of the normal routines with the rest of the club."

Jack paused and then asked the burning question: "Ozzie, you are one of the best—perhaps *the* best—infielder in the history of the game. You've won a ton of Gold Gloves and you're voted onto the All-Star team year after year. So why do you feel the need to take all of this extra practice everyday?"

Ozzie looked at Jack and said something very profound. "Jack, it's quite simple. I can't afford to have to think. If I have to think about where the ball is going to go for even a split second after the ball leaves the hitter's bat, then that ball will get by me, and I can't afford to let that happen—ever. It's all about reflex."

Are you ready to commit to practicing at the level that Ozzie did? If you are, the new habits you need to master are described right here in this book. So read on, but not before you take time out to master the art of counter-intuitive selling with The Successful Seven action steps for this chapter.

The Successful Seven: Chapter 2
Action Steps for Mastering the Art of Counter-Intuitive Selling

1. Realize that nothing will change in your sales career (or with any of your current habits) without the amount of practice required to transform an existing habit into a new one.

2. Understand that **habits are hard to break** and hard to develop, and that doing so requires periods of planned repetitive practice.

3. Even if you are at the top of your sales game today, commit to setting aside time every day to practice the new habits described in each chapter of *Counter-Intuitive Selling*.

4. Designate a sales buddy or a mentor/manager who will check in with you every day to ask you if you are following through with your practice commitments.

5. Always practice a new habit for **21 days** before attempting to use your new behavior in a critical selling situation.

6. During your practice periods, always practice your new habits in **noncritical selling situations** (with low-risk customers, team members, or your manager).

7. Have patience with yourself! Changing habits, especially old ones and bad ones, isn't easy—but *you can do it*!

chapter three

How It Feels at First—*and What to Do About It*

Trying counter-intuitive ways of doing things will
definitely feel uncomfortable at first. Knowing this is
the first step toward real success.

This chapter is all about thinking. It is about the importance of the thought process—your thought process—as you enter the world of counter-intuitive selling. Let's begin by returning to Ken and his first steps with the concepts of counter-intuitive selling.

Ken had been practicing one of the key counter-intuitive techniques for about three weeks. He was about to get on the phone for the first time to use it (you'll discover in Chapter 20 exactly what "it" is) with critical prospects. Before he made the call, he walked over to my desk, looked at me, drew a big sigh, and shared what was on his mind. "I'm not sure I'm ready for this. It is so different and so foreign to what I've always done. It doesn't seem natural."

Ken was ready, but inside himself, he did not feel ready. Counter-intuitive selling was not feeling natural to him. In other words, he was feeling uncomfortable—kind of like we feel when we try to fold our arms the "other" way. His reluctance was natural, but it was vital to Ken's future success that he and I engage in the "Swiss watchmaker thinking" conversation. It was the last critical conversation Ken and I needed to have before he actually moved from practicing in safe situations to practicing counter-intuitive selling in the real world.

Shifting Paradigms

Let's think about what is happening to Ken, because it also will happen to you as you journey deeper into counter-intuitive selling. The easy stuff comes first, and he was starting to step into the realm of the difficult. In counter-intuitive selling, the difficulty starts with execution.

It all goes back to having a real commitment to change as an individual, to being willing to do whatever it takes to make change stick. That commitment, which we touched on in Chapter 1, is critical at this point in the process.

Even after sustained practice of new behaviors and working to transform these new behaviors into our new habits, we will be, whether we realize it or not, pulled by our old habits. We will be pulled into feeling comfortable with the old ways of doing things. At times, we will find ourselves running back to these old ways, even if they were not producing results for us.

Why would we do this?

Valuable Lessons from the Watchmakers

To help Ken find the answer to that question, I told him the old story about the famous Swiss watchmakers. These highly skilled craftsmen had dominated the world of watchmaking for centuries, but lost a huge part of their market to a new breed of watchmakers who didn't have old habits that stopped them from thinking in different ways about making watches.

In the 1970s, the Swiss, who all but owned the watchmaking industry, were busy in their multibillion-dollar research labs looking for new and less expensive ways to build watches with higher quality and more precision.

Meanwhile, Japanese watchmakers came along and introduced the transistorized watch, which quickly took over a large part of the watch market. Within a few short years, the Swiss had lost their dominance of the watch market. While they continue to have a large share of the high-end watch market, the Swiss have never been able to gain back the bulk of the total watch market that they allowed the Japanese (and now others) to steal away.

What happened?

Some people call it a paradigm shift. *Paradigm* is defined as a pattern that is followed, often without questioning the thinking or rationale behind it. The paradigm that the Swiss watchmakers were following was this: a watch must have moving parts. Because the transistor did not fit their paradigm about watches, they couldn't even imagine a watch without moving parts. Therefore, a large portion of the market they once dominated is now owned by others.

Even after the transistorized watch movement had taken hold and the Japanese were continuing to take away a larger share of the market, some of the Swiss watchmakers remained in denial. In their minds they must have been thinking that what the Japanese had developed couldn't really be a watch because it didn't have moving parts.

Not only was it a watch, it was a more accurate watch and a more durable watch. Today, even some of the most prominent Swiss watch companies use Japanese movements or Japanese electronic components in many of their watches.

Is this what you want to see happen in your sales career? Do you want to see a large part of your market taken by others who can think differently about sales? If so, then simply put this book down and continue doing what you have always done to get results. (But remember our definition of insanity in the first chapter.)

Changing Habits to Change Results

Why is it that we think we have to say or do certain things in a certain way in the sales process? Is it because our own past thinking, actions, and learning stop us from embracing new ways to approach situations? Because we've always been taught to do things, such as share our name at the beginning of a phone call with a prospect or demo our product when we have enough interest, we continue to do these things. We don't repeat these behaviors and habits because they give us the best results. As a matter of fact, we continue them even when we know that they *don't* give us the best results. We struggle to get out of a paradigm that is not working, and it is very difficult to do this!

If you are ready to change your thinking about sales and then your behavior, continue to read this book. Realize, however, that many of the proven ideas and techniques shared in the remainder of this book will question your paradigms (your beliefs and habits) about sales. At first, these new ideas will feel unnatural and uncomfortable. But, remember one thing as you continue your journey: **feeling uncomfortable is good, and it leads to success.**

Before you move on to the next chapter, be sure to complete The Successful Seven from this chapter.

The Successful Seven: Chapter 3
Action Steps for Mastering the Art of Counter-Intuitive Selling

1. Do not allow "Swiss watchmaker thinking" to paralyze your ability to change your habits and adopt counter-intuitive selling behaviors.

2. Realize and accept that **new behaviors of counter-intuitive selling will not feel comfortable** when you first begin to execute in the real world.

3. Thinking differently and allowing your mind to think differently are keys to success with counter-intuitive selling.

4. When you catch yourself slipping back into old ways of doing things, **return to practicing** to improve your ability to execute on the necessary changes.

5. If you are a sales manager, be sure to share the "Swiss watchmaker thinking" story with your team members as they transition from the world of practicing to the world of living counter-intuitive selling.

6. If you are an individual sales professional, be sure to reread this chapter when you are ready to move from the world of counter-intuitive practice to the real world of customers and prospects.

7. Most importantly, **be patient with yourself** and rely on your "sales buddy" (refer to step 4 in The Successful Seven in Chapter 2) to help you stay on track. Talk at least once a day, every day with your sales buddy.

chapter four

Consistency in Repetition Builds New Habits—*and* *Makes New Habits Stick!*

Get into a new pattern of practice that leads to a new pattern of
success. The appointments you set with yourself
become the most important appointments that you
ever place into your calendar.

Everyone on the team noticed the changes in Ken. When he
walked into our meetings there was an air of confidence that came with
him. As we talked with him, we got the sense that he had become a person who controls his time, rather than allowing his time to control him.

This was a big change from the Ken of just a few months earlier.
Back then, Ken was one of those salespeople who jumped at any potential appointment he could put into his calendar. Now he was in
charge, and he decided with whom he would meet, and even more
importantly, when he would meet with them (more on this later in
Chapter 38). Even more significant was the fact that his prospects and
customers respected him more.

The change in Ken was all about how he controls his time, and
how he sets appointments with himself that he will not break for anyone. **This means anyone**. It all started when Ken realized that the most
important appointments he sets are the ones he sets with himself.

Ken was a skeptic at first, like most other salespeople. He just
could not comprehend the potential value of what we refer to as
"**I-Team**" appointments. These are the appointments that you set

with yourself—the ones that need to stay on your calendar and do not move for anyone or anything that might tempt you to do so.

In mastering the art of counter-intuitive selling, Ken had the same challenge that you now face. In fact, he had the same challenge that all salespeople face when attempting to master the art of the un-expected—realizing that **habits only change over time**.

Changing Habits Through Time-Spaced Repetition

This chapter is about how to change your current behaviors. We talked in Chapter 2 about how long it takes for you to establish the habits, both good and bad, that make up your behavior patterns to-day. Your habits are so ingrained that, for the most part, you aren't even aware of the behavior until after it occurs. Your behavior is reflex (remember Ozzie Smith?); you don't even think before you react with your habitual behavior.

Have you ever been on a sales call and said something in response to the prospect, only to say to yourself later, "I *knew* I should have an-swered that question differently!" Intellectually, you knew there was a better response, but based on your ingrained habits, you responded instinctively. Your habits forced you to answer in that specific way. Knowing that you should respond more effectively—and actually re-sponding that way—are two different things.

There is only one way to change your habits, and change your habits permanently. It comes through something called **time-spaced repetition** (which I mentioned in Chapter 1).

What is time-spaced repetition? Simply defined, it is continual, reg-ular practice of a new behavior over an extended period. We've already established that it takes at least 21 days to change a habit or behavior. How do you ensure that you do what you need to do in those 21 days to impact change? This is where the I-Team appointments are critical.

In order to change your ineffective sales habits, you must estab-lish one of the most important new habits that you will acquire as you master the art of counter-intuitive selling: setting and keeping your I-

Team appointments. Acquiring this habit also requires another skill that is essential for success in counter-intuitive selling—discipline.

Almost every salesperson struggles with the I-Team appointment concept at first. They ask, "Why should I set appointments with myself when my time needs to be spent in front of customers?" The truth is simple: **if you do not get out of your old habits and establish new ones, your results will not improve**. Breaking old habits takes time, discipline, and *time-spaced repetition*.

Once you establish your consistent calendar of appointments with yourself and stick to it (remember, these do not change for any reason!), you will begin to notice significant changes in your behavior and then in your results.

How do you get started?

Begin by opening your appointment book or electronic calendar and scheduling short, 30 to 45-minute appointments with yourself every other day. Try to keep the appointments around the same time, when you believe you will experience the least amount of potential disruption. Once these are set, create the mindset that these are appointments with your most important customer (in reality, you are your most important customer!) that cannot be broken.

If someone wants to meet with you during your scheduled I-Team appointments, simply respond, "My apologies. I have a call with one of my top clients at that time. Can we schedule this for 45 minutes later than the time you suggested?" Nine times out of ten, this will be all that you need to do to keep your I-Team time secure. In the rare situations where this approach does not work, then simply make the change, and move your I-Team appointment time back 45 minutes. This way, you keep your time on the calendar and you accommodate the urgent request from the other person for your time.

Getting the Most from I-Team Appointments

Once you have the time on your calendar, what is next?

The next step is to map out your habit-changing activities that will fill this time on your calendar on an every-other-day basis. At first, use the time to read this book and act on the *The Successful Seven* at the end of each chapter. As you move further along in this book, your I-Team appointment time will be used to practice your new habits *before* you put them into action with live/critical prospects and customers.

The essentially important success factor at this stage is establishing your I-Team time and committing to maintaining the schedule, no matter what. This is the first critical step toward changing your habits. It will be both challenging and rewarding at the same time:

- *Challenging,* in that you need the discipline to stick with your schedule and your plan, which is not always easy.
- *Rewarding,* in that once you stick to your plan for about three weeks, you will begin to feel your new habits materializing. Once you get about two or three months into your recurring I-Team appointments, you will begin to wonder how you ever got along without this self-development time.

Here are some tips regarding the best time of the day to schedule your recurring I-Team appointments. As you move through counter-intuitive selling, you will quickly realize that some of your most critical prime selling time is different than what you think it is today. Initially, you might be thinking that your I-Team time can be scheduled early in the morning or at the end of the day. I am going to suggest that you do not take this approach. (Trust me, you will buy into this later in the book.)

Look for time during the normal course of the day to schedule your appointments with yourself. This way, as you discover all of the counter-intuitive reasons why this is the best time to hold your I-Team meetings, you'll appreciate the fact that these can stay where they are on your calendar. The consensus among all of the salespeople that master counter-intuitive selling is that the best recurring I-Team appointment time is midmorning or midafternoon.

Laying the Groundwork for Success

We've covered the importance of changing your current selling habits along with the need to establish a process and discipline for achieving new results. Next, we need to move on to the important task of asking yourself tough questions about the results you have achieved to this point in your career.

Before you begin reading the next section of the book, though, it is time to take important action that will change your selling career. As you act on The Successful Seven, take a moment to review your action steps and progress from Chapters 1 through 4. Do not start Part Two of this book until you are satisfied that you have laid the **groundwork for success**.

As you continue through this book and step into the world of counter-intuitive selling, keep the following in mind: your I-Team appointments and meetings are some of the most critical activities and a necessary and integral part of mastering "the art of the unexpected." Without these important meetings, you will never truly become a counter-intuitive selling professional.

The Successful Seven: Chapter 4
Action Steps for Mastering the Art of Counter-Intuitive Selling

1. Accept the reality that habits only change over time. **Commit to a calendar of time to practice changing your old and ineffective habits**.

2. Embrace the concept of **setting appointments with yourself** on an every-other-day schedule. Refer to these as **I-Team appointments**.

3. Make the commitment to yourself that your I-Team appointments **do not change** for anyone or anything.

4. If you absolutely must change the time of an I-Team appointment, reschedule it to immediately follow the cause of the interruption— **keep it booked on your calendar.**

5. Schedule your I-Team appointments for midmorning or midafternoon, and immediately schedule out those appointments for the next six months.

6. Plan out the topic/habit areas of focus for your I-Team appointments at least two weeks in advance, *and do not leave a topic area until you notice progress in your results.*

7. To prepare for success in the upcoming section of this book, review the action steps from the first four chapters and complete any unfinished action steps.

How to Get Started

Harnessing your
experiences and your
learning power
into your
personal success system

chapter five

BEWARE!

The "Reason to Believe"
Why You Lost a Deal Is
Probably Not the <u>Real</u> Reason

The counter-intuitive sales professional quickly comes to the realization that there is more hiding behind the reason for a lost sale than the customer shares.

How many times have you accepted "price" as the reason for losing a piece of business? How recently in the past have you accepted this as the reason for not winning a deal? Although price may be the reason the customer shares with you, and although that may be the reason you believe you lost the business, the counter-intuitive selling professional learns to think otherwise. To explore this important concept, let's go back to an earlier time in our sales group's history, before Ken had mastered the art of counter-intuitive selling.

We started our weekly meeting by talking about the "wins" of the week and patted each other on the back about the business we just closed. Once we were done with what is one of the biggest rituals that most salespeople go through on a regular basis, it was time to get on to the real meeting—the harder part of the meeting. It was time to get to the **lost-business review**.

Ken, who had not yet entered the world of counter-intuitive selling, was the first up. "We lost PSG to our usual competitor, and we clearly lost it on price. When our competitor came back at the last minute with some huge price concessions, it pretty much put us out of the running, even though we definitely had the better business solution for PSG."

Is this starting to sound all too familiar? Do you find yourself sharing explanations similar to Ken's with your sales manager or convincing yourself of this reasoning? If so, then we have some good news and some bad news. Let's start with the bad news.

In these situations, we tend to fall into a line of thinking that allows us to **justify in our own mind** that "price" was the real issue, and that we did everything else right. We convince ourselves that in the end we lost the deal on price. In doing so, we let ourselves off the hook in a big way, *and we let some big deals slip away in the process.*

This line of thinking really damages the sales careers of many potential high performers. Even worse, it turns those who could be outstanding performers into average performers. Blaming lost sales on price issues alone is one of the most common blind spots that kill sales careers *before* a salesperson has the opportunity to enter the world of counter-intuitive selling.

Losing the Deal: The Call

Let's go into Ken's selling scenario with PSG a little deeper, and let's get to a real moment of truth.

Ken's phone rang as he was getting into his car to head to his first appointment of the day. He recognized the number, and answered the call with great anticipation.

"Good morning, Jack," he answered, before Jack had even said a word. "How's everything shaping up for the move to the new facility? I just passed it on my way home yesterday, and I can't believe the progress!"

After a few minutes of the usual small talk, Ken's mood began to change dramatically. It started as Jack steered the conversation to business. "Ken, I wanted to call you as soon as I received word this morning," Jack began. "It turns out that the other potential vendor for this project came back early yesterday with some price concessions that were pretty significant."

When he paused, Ken was speechless.

"Actually, Ken, the price concessions were *really* significant. So significant that it got everyone's attention, and evidently the decision was reached last night to go with their proposal. Although I'm surprised, I can't say that I disagree with the decision. I know that your solution better fits our needs, and I think the others do as well. But, business is business and price is price."

Ken did what most sales professionals do in this situation; he entered the price game as well. After all, what else could he do? He started to talk rather than just continue to listen. "Jack, give me about an hour and I'll be back to you. I am quite sure we can also provide the same price concessions."

When Ken heard Jack's next comments, he knew the game was over.

"Ken, I thought you would be able to, but the decision's been made and I was told that it is time to move on and get rolling. I didn't want it to turn out this way, and I feel kind of embarrassed right now, as I've been leading this project. Rest assured, there are more projects on the way, and next time, I'll make sure you are positioned to get the business."

Once the conversation ended, Ken began to think about what had just happened. What did Jack mean when he said "next time, I'll make sure you are positioned to get the business"? Ken was positioned to get *this* business, according to Jack. At least that is what Jack kept saying along the way.

Was Jack lying?

Because Ken was not yet a student of counter-intuitive selling, there was not much else that he could do, except to believe his own "stinkin' thinkin'" as motivational author and speaker Zig Ziglar would say. Ken was on his way to convincing himself, along with his sales manager, that this deal was absolutely lost on price.

What do you think?

Let's follow the trail of this selling situation a little further.

Ken had been engaged in the selling process with PSG for the past nine months. His updates in our weekly meetings were convincing. He could answer any questions that I asked him about the account with legitimate-sounding answers, and he usually answered with conviction.

Somewhere along the way, however, Ken fell into one of the worst **sales career–killing traps**. He moved from "active selling" mode into "waiting for the deal to close" mode, convinced that this deal was his to lose. In the end he was absolutely right; the deal was absolutely his to lose, ***and he lost it!*** By believing all of the "reasons to believe" that his prospect was telling him, Ken was destroying his sales career, lost deal by lost deal, and he didn't even realize it.

There are solid reasons why Jack lost this deal. As you continue your journey through the world of counter-intuitive selling, you will discover the real reasons why Jack lost this deal. (<u>HINT</u>: price is not one of the reasons.) What is more important is that you will learn how to make sure you never again lose a deal the way this deal (and the way probably many of your deals) was lost.

Using the Lost-Business Review to See Beyond the "Reason to Believe"

The really sad news is that price becomes the "reason to believe." It certainly became the reason Ken believed, and as he passed it along it became the reason for his manager to believe. Eventually, it became the reason for everyone in the company to believe. When everyone believed, it took *everyone* off the hook. Everyone believed the "stinkin' thinkin'" that **this deal was lost on price**.

What we have here is a typical case of salesperson misinformation spreading throughout the company like wildfire. In the end, this is one of the most damaging traits that destroys otherwise great sales forces. That's the bad news.

The good news is that when you complete your journey through counter-intuitive selling and you have mastered the art of the unexpected, you will be fully equipped to handle this situation. You can make sure that you never again attempt to convince yourself and others, as Ken did so well with PSG, that you lost a deal on price when **it was not the real reason** for losing the sale. Even more important to your career, you will know how to head off this situation, and others like it, before they start to head down this slippery slope.

Questions to Ask During Your Lost Business Review

The key to your lost business review is objectivity. In order to attain objectivity, it will be important to talk to others about the lost business. The best person to talk to is the customer—preferably the actual decision-maker. Until we hear the truth from the customer, we are only guessing at the real reasons why we lost the business.

How you position this conversation with the customer will be the key to gaining an accurate summary of why you lost the business. Your conversation with the customer should sound something like this:

"Jack, I appreciate the fact that you made a decision to award your business to someone else—and I also respect this decision. My goal is to learn from this experience and to fully understand why and how we lost your business. I value your thoughts and advice, and I will use your advice to improve in the future. Whatever you can share with me will be greatly appreciated."

Once you share this with the lost customer, it is important to focus on some of the following questions:

- Were we ever under serious consideration to win your business?
- If so, what occurred that eliminated us from the competition?
- As you look at our dialog and meetings with you and your team as opposed to those of the company that won your business, what was the difference?

- Did your decision surround the actual solution, or did it have more to do with each company and the teams representing each company?
- Did you have the confidence that we would deliver what we represented during our meetings and dialog?
- Did what we present as a solution actually match your business need?
- What do you feel is the most important lesson that I can learn from this experience?
- Do you have any other advice for me as someone who would like to have the opportunity to do business with you in the future?
- Have you actually awarded the business to someone else?

I recommend that you have this conversation with the customer in the time period between 2-4 weeks after learning that you lost the business. I recommend that you call the customer to request a face-to-face meeting to delve into your questions, if this is possible. If you request the meeting too soon, your prospect may believe that you are trying to change their decision, and he or she may not grant you the meeting. If you wait too long, the situation and circumstances may not be clear in your prospect's mind.

Your mindset for this meeting should be to ask short questions and do a lot of listening. When conducted regularly in all situations in which you lose business, these meetings will become invaluable to your future success.

It's All About Realization

I want to make sure that as you continue on your journey you learn along the way. A major part of learning and mastering counter-intuitive selling is what I call **realization**, and this chapter is all about realization. Realization is the first step toward change. If you've had a few "aha!" or "Wow, that's me!" moments as you read this chapter, you're definitely on the right track.

Remember, mastering the art of counter-intuitive selling does not happen overnight. Laying the groundwork to make permanent changes to your selling habits takes time. Before you move on to the next chapter, it is time to put some counter-intuitive action steps to work for you. It is time to take a close look at the deals you recently lost. It is time for some personal realization.

The lost-business review is one of your most powerful counter-intuitive tools, but only if you are willing to be honest with yourself.

The Successful Seven: Chapter 5
Action Steps for Mastering the Art of Counter-Intuitive Selling

1. Make **lost-business reviews** a regular part of your sales process. Follow the process outlined in this chapter.

2. Use Ken's story about Jack and PSG as an example of the **"reason to believe" trap** to gauge your level of "stinkin' thinkin'" when it comes to lost business.

3. Gather all of the information you have available on the last five deals that you lost.

4. Retrace your steps in the sales process for each of these lost deals, and chart out **where the deal went bad**.

5. Look for patterns in when you received word that the business was not coming to you—especially where you **moved from "active selling" mode to "waiting for the deal to close" mode**.

6. Use the realizations (the "ahas") that you experience during your lost-business review as **signals to look for similar danger points** as you pursue other deals.

7. If you are committed to never again lose a deal based on "the reason to believe," study the rest of *Counter-Intuitive Selling* and **follow all of the action steps** at the end of every chapter.

chapter six

"Going to the Balcony" to Gain Greater Perspective

The power of "going to the balcony" to gain another perspective adds to the power of counter-intuitive thinking. Master this, and you enter a new world of selling.

Now, let's move forward once again, to a time when Ken had been working with the major pharmaceutical company, Zucor, for about six months. As he continued to review in his mind the last few meetings with the company, he knew there was more to what he was reliving and rethinking; *he just couldn't put his finger on it.* The more he thought about it, the more he kept replaying the same events and outcomes in his mind. He finally realized that he needed a better view and perspective. It was time for Ken to "go to the balcony" to see the situation in an entirely different light.

As sales professionals, many times we are just too close to the situation to gain the insight that we need. We are too "locked in" and we only see the situation from one point of view or one perspective—*ours.*

In many selling situations, we are the only one from our team on the call with the customer. We don't always have the luxury of another set of eyes and ears. In these situations, it is vital for us to engage in counter-intuitive thinking. This is where "going to the balcony" comes into play.

Ken was about to take this step, and in doing so, significantly increase his effectiveness.

Capturing Critical Information

When Ken entered the world of counter-intuitive selling, he had quickly realized the power of adding two new items to his notes during any meeting with a client or a prospect: the participant list *and* the seating diagram. He began to wonder how he ever made progress without these two pieces of vital information (these tools also play a vital role in *the power of visualization,* a counter-intuitive technique you learn more about in the next chapter).

Ken wanted to make sure that he captured all of the information he needed during each customer meeting, so he created the following list that he carries in his Day-Timer:

1. Commit to always taking notes at every meeting with any prospect and customer.
2. Make sure that the notes include a listing of all meeting participants.
3. Be sure to draw a diagram of the meeting indicating the seating position of all participants.
4. As the meeting progresses, list the events as things unfold, and number them in chronological order.
5. Date all notes from the meeting, and be sure to note the start time and the end time of the meeting.
6. Highlight significant statements by indicating the person who expresses these points.
7. Note the contributors from the prospect or customer who become spokespersons for the customer's team.
8. Note any participants that leave early or arrive late, and note the exact times of these arrivals and departures.
9. Capture all action steps agreed upon during the meeting, including the date and time of the next meeting.

Going to the Balcony

As Ken got ready for this most critical step in counter-intuitive selling, he was excited to gain the additional perspective. He made sure he had all of his notes, especially the diagram of the meeting and the meeting participant list.

To help clear his thinking and avoid any distractions, Ken moved to another space in the office. He chose an area that no one used these days (one of the best types of places you can possibly find to "go to the balcony"), so he knew no one would know how or where to find him. He turned off his cell phone, left his laptop at his desk, and headed down the hallway.

In the unused office area, Ken dropped his notes and file on an empty table, headed to the window, and sat on the floor, where he took five minutes to just clear his head. He thought about something totally unrelated to what he was about to review—about the car he had admired on the way to the office this morning and the storm from the previous night. He just wanted to think about anything other than work at the moment, so he could clear his mind.

Once he did this, he went back to the table to review his notes from the meeting and his file on the prospect. Thinking back to the last meeting with Zucor, he placed his diagram on the table in front of him, positioning it so that he was in the exact position at this table that he had been in when the meeting took place.

Next, he picked up his detailed notes on exactly what had taken place and when each event occurred during the meeting. He was extremely glad that he had the events listed in order, as it easily allowed him to re-create the meeting.

Ken wanted to do more than remember the meeting, however; he wanted to relive it. The goal of "going to the balcony" is to relive the meeting from a more distant perspective, and the meeting room diagram allowed Ken to do this. As Ken stared at the diagram of the room, he stood up so he could begin to sense his distance from the room where the meeting took place and from the actual events, to gain a new perspective.

With his notes, he stepped back through each event, from the minute the meeting began. As Ken went through this process, he looked at the meeting from a third-person perspective. His diagram that showed the participants, including him, allowed him to do this. The questions he asked himself and the answers he received began to point to something significant.

The light bulb went off in his head. The answers he was receiving were not the answers he needed. He immediately understood why; someone was missing from the meeting! Ken realized, through the power of "going to the balcony," that he needed to involve another group of key people from Zucor in his next meeting with the group.

"Going to the balcony" provided Ken with a perspective that was nearly impossible for him to gain while he was in the meeting as an active participant. The ability to place himself in the position of a distant observer by "going to the balcony" had become extremely powerful and rewarding to Ken. This was not the first time it paid off.

This time, however, had the potential to pay off big. The opportunity at Zucor was large—multimillion and multiyear. Ken could not wait until the next morning, when he planned to phone his key contact at Zucor.

Acting on a New Perspective

In his car early the next morning, Ken dialed the Zucor number. Helen, his main contact was already in her office, as she always was. Ken was always impressed with the way Helen started her day, and today it was about to pay off big for both of them.

"Helen, how are things this morning? I was thinking about you and our last meeting as I left the office last night, and I realized something."

Helen told him that not only was she appreciative that Ken called before her day got away from her and she couldn't take his call, but she also was interested in what he was thinking.

"In our last meeting, I let you and the rest of the Zucor team down by carrying on discussions that we shouldn't have had. As I think about it, we really need to gain the perspective of the business unit leaders. We shouldn't think about holding our next meeting without including them."

Ken waited for Helen's response. After she thought for a minute, she said. "Ken, you're absolutely right. Thanks for thinking about them. When we hang up, I'll check to see which ones are available next Tuesday, when our meeting is set. If they can't attend, I'll let you know so we can reschedule for a time when they are here and can join us."

Then Helen added the comment that was most significant to Ken. "Thanks for thinking this through. I don't know why I didn't think of it, but I am sure glad you did. We would have ended up just meeting again after our next meeting, because in the end we need their buy-in. I really appreciate the way you think about things."

By "going to the balcony," Ken had just solidified the soon-to-be-closed deal with Zucor. The next meeting would have an expanded audience from the Zucor team, and he was confident that this would push the deal over the finish line.

This was only half of the mental preparation that Ken needed for the meeting with Zucor. However; the remainder would focus on the morning of the next meeting. Thanks to the insights he gained from his trip to the balcony, Ken was ready for that next vital step.

The Successful Seven: Chapter 6
Action Steps for Mastering the Art of Counter-Intuitive Selling

1. Commit to **always take notes at every meeting** you conduct with any prospect or customer. (*Use the list inside this chapter as a guideline for the information you need to capture in your notes.*) These notes will be essential to review when "going to the balcony."

2. Use the power of "going to the balcony" to **gain additional insight** that you cannot gain during the actual live meeting.

3. When "going to the balcony," do so in a quiet place and make sure you remove all potential distractions (turn off your cell phone, for example).

4. Once you arrive in the quiet place, take at least five minutes to **completely clear your mind** before you begin your "going to the balcony" process.

5. While "going to the balcony," **relive the meeting exactly as it took place**: use your diagram to re-create the seating positions of all participants and use your notes to re-create the chronology of events.

6. Based on what you learn during your "going to the balcony" experience, **create a list of action steps** for the account.

7. Once your action steps are solid in your mind, **immediately call your main contact** in the account to gain his or her reaction and thoughts on your findings.

chapter seven

Creating Your Success in Your Mind: The Power of Visualization

---

In the world of counter-intuitive selling, your ability to create a mental image of your success before it happens creates the mental edge you need.

The morning of his next meeting with Zucor, Ken was up extra early. He had made sure that everything else on his calendar or his urgent to-do list was under control. If it wasn't, it could wait. He had cleared the deck the evening before, so he could focus solely on his meeting with Zucor.

Ken began by reviewing all of his notes from all of his meetings with Zucor, paying special attention to the participant lists and the meeting diagrams. He laid out each diagram and each corresponding participant list in chronological order, up to and including the meeting two weeks ago.

As he relived each of the meetings, he noticed patterns within each meeting as well as within the meetings as a whole. One thing he immediately picked up on was that the Zucor team usually sat in a similar pattern. Another trend he noticed was that the same two or three individuals usually started and ended the meeting with their comments. It was clear that certain individuals carried the bulk of the dialog for Zucor.

There was one person who, although he was not at each of the meetings, had been in the very first one. When Ken compared the prior meeting participant lists to the one of the participants for today's meeting, he discovered something interesting: *this* individual was the key business unit leader that Helen, his main contact, had made sure would be in attendance today. Ken's notes indicated that when this individual was in the meeting, he carried the bulk of the dialog for Zucor and that many of the other participants looked to him to decide what to do next in the meeting.

Ken was on to something. He would use his new information to help visualize the flow and outcome of today's meeting with Zucor.

The Power of Visualization Comes Alive

Ken needed his mind to be as clear as possible, so he:

- put everything away except for the file on Zucor and the other material he needed to prepare for the meeting,
- sat at a table that represented the table for the meeting later in the day where he could "see" in his mind where each participant might be seated, and
- visualized the entire meeting as he believed it would progress— and as he wanted it to progress.

Ken was getting a clearer picture, so he started to imagine today's meeting. He began visualizing the flow of the meeting. He planned to include all Zucor participants in the dialog. Ken would always look to the business unit leader (and Helen) for confirmation or for signs that he needed to provide more proof and validation that he could deliver on the needs of the business.

In other words, in Ken's mind, the "movie" of the impending meeting was produced and previewed by Ken.

A critical part of Ken's visualization preparation was the review of and preparation for any of the potential objections that could be raised by any member of the Zucor team. Ken's notes from previous meetings included this information, and he reviewed all of it carefully. He was not about to be tripped up by an unexpected objection—not at this point in the game. His detailed notes from the previous meetings provided him with all of the ammunition he needed to creatively think of and review any other potential objections—and, most importantly, the answers he would need. He even went as far as to look at his notes from meetings with companies that had profiles similar to Zucor's, to see if any other potential objections should be added to the list and their answers visualized. He wanted to make sure that he covered all of the bases.

Why was the objection visualization such a critical and important part of this preparation? If you have forgotten it by now, head back to Chapter 2 and relive the Ozzie Smith story of fielding ground balls before each game. It will quickly remind you of the need to make sure your responses to potential objections become reflex. *You cannot afford to have to stop and think about how you will respond in the heat of battle. The minute you stop to think, the battle will be lost.*

When Ken completed the potential objection visualization, he moved on to visualizing more of the overall dialog and flow of the meeting. He pulled out the agenda for the meeting (he had worked with Helen to get her input and buy-in on this). As he moved through the agenda, he visualized who would be responding and how he would interact with the group. He even visualized key pauses and the questions he would pose or the person that he would turn to from Zucor to share his or her thoughts at that time.

At one point, Ken visualized the potential most challenging moments of the meeting and how he would handle these. Visualizing the worst-case scenarios prepared Ken to remain calm, collected, and in control of both the meeting and himself. Ken knows from experience that being prepared mentally is the most important component in the battle for success. Once he harnessed his emotions and his reactions to the worst that could possibly happen in the meeting, he felt more in control of himself.

Achieving Clarity: The Final Replay

It was clear from the meeting notes and the most recent meeting with Zucor that the business unit leader who participated in the first meeting and was now joining today's meeting would play a key role. Ken's visualization began to focus on this individual and how he would use his counter-intuitive selling to gain agreement and confidence with this individual. Ken played the movie of the meeting that was about to happen over and over in his mind, focusing his instant replay on the critical points of interaction with the business unit leader.

Once he believed that he had these key moments fully orchestrated into his visualization, Ken replayed the entire movie in his mind one more time. Before he did, however, Ken once again reviewed all of the previous meetings' notes and diagrams. One by one, he took a final look at each participant list and meeting diagram, along with the corresponding notes from each meeting. He started with the first meeting and ended with the meeting that occurred two weeks ago.

Ken was feeling more and more confident about his approach, his questions, and his objection review. He was now ready for the final visualization replay. Ken closed his eyes, took a deep breath, waited about 30 seconds, and then let the movie begin to play. This time, he allowed his mind to replay the movie in widescreen, enabling his perspective to grow so he would be able to look for anything on the peripheral as well as at the center of his focus.

Ken was ready. As he went to his car, he walked with confidence. He was going to win today, and Zucor was going to win as well. He was excited and ready to succeed, and it showed. Ken was poised and prepared to bring home a large piece of business.

The Successful Seven: Chapter 7
Action Steps for Mastering the Art of Counter-Intuitive Selling

1. A few hours before your next meeting with any critical high-potential prospect or customer, **clear your deck of urgent to-dos, e-mail, and phone messages**.

2. **Collect your notes, diagrams, and participant lists** from all of your previous meetings with this customer or prospect. Also grab the **files of customers with similar profiles** to this target customer.

3. Head to a place where you can **work in solitude without interruption**, and lay out all of the meeting diagrams and corresponding participant lists in chronological order.

4. Position yourself where you can look at the information and **relive the chronological order** and flow of each meeting.

5. **Prepare for any and all potential objections** that will possibly enter the dialog of today's meeting. Visualize the worst possible outcomes, and prepare to respond to these.

6. Focus the remainder of your visualization on the **desired outcome of the meeting** and the major dialog participants from the prospect or customer's team.

7. Visualize moving the meeting to your desired outcomes and how you will close the meeting. Do this several times until you **feel in control and comfortable**.

chapter eight

Beginning to Plant the Needed Behavioral Change Triggers

Successfully moving into the world of counter-intuitive selling
requires practice and conditioning, and conditioning takes
behavioral triggers.

You've seen how Ken used some of the most critical techniques of counter-intuitive selling to move toward success with a major account. As you begin to make initial progress toward entering the world of counter-intuitive selling, it is vital that you also learn to create reminders or triggers that will force your needed behavioral changes into action. Without taking this vital step of creating triggers, none of your new behaviors will take hold. None of these new behaviors will become habits, and none of your new behaviors will establish what is referred to as "stickiness."

The reality is that thoughts are thoughts and action is action. Some of you may start to think that I am beginning to play with semantics, but I am not, so let me repeat this critical statement: **thoughts are thoughts and actions are actions**. You can think something all you want. You can read and reread this book as many times as you want. As a matter of fact, you can go ahead and read this book a hundred times and chances are that, with all that reading alone, nothing will change in your sales career. Nothing will change, that is, until you take action. If you're like most human beings, you need some triggers to remind you to take different action than you have taken until now. This process is commonly referred to as *situational behavioral change*.

To be successful in establishing triggers, you must discipline yourself to take the needed action that will lead to behavioral change. Are you confused at this point? If so, don't worry; that's normal and to be expected. This chapter explains to you how to understand and use behavioral triggers, and their overall importance to your success in entering and *remaining* in the world of counter-intuitive selling. Here, you'll find some examples of behavioral triggers that are proven to work in the world of counter-intuitive selling.

The triggers you use will have one purpose: to remind you to act differently. As you practice a new behavior, it soon becomes a new habit. Until behaviors become habits, you will have to think about acting the new way every time you want to act differently (remember the arm-folding exercise from Chapter 2?). If you need to revisit the **21-day reality of forming new habits**, take a minute to review Chapter 2 before you continue. The key point to remember is this: you don't have to think about a behavior once it has become a habit.

Through many years of training sales professionals in the art of counter-intuitive selling, there is one fact I have found that continues to ring true. The sales professionals that embrace the use of behavioral triggers are the ones that end up mastering "the art of the unexpected." The salespeople that choose to pass up the triggers and not put them to use, thinking that triggers are either silly or a waste of time, are the ones that never quite get to the next level in their sales career. The choice is yours.

Over the years, I have learned that the most effective behavioral triggers are the simple ones. As we step back into Ken's world, we will see this truth at work as he moves through a typical day in the life of the sales professional learning to reap the benefits of counter-intuitive selling.

How Behavior Triggers Work

When Ken awoke this morning, his mind was on the major calls he needed to place to high-potential prospects, and the major meeting he had today with one of his largest customers of the past few years.

The note hanging on his bathroom mirror hit him between the eyes. Three simple words were written on the note:

> **shower**
> **visualize**
> **Zucor**

This note serves one purpose. Can you figure it out? If you guessed that this is Ken's trigger to visualize during his morning shower the critical Zucor meeting that will take place later today, you are correct.

Now you might be wondering, why does Ken need this note to himself? Won't he remember this without the note?

Chances are Ken will have a million other things on his mind as he awakes, including anything he dreamed about while he was sleeping and anything that pops into his mind as he heads to the shower. His normal morning habit may be to grab his cell phone to check the time and his messages. While he does this, chances are pretty high that he will get distracted by a message or a call and his mind will not remain focused on visualizing the Zucor meeting.

Ken's goal for using his trigger is to make sure that, no matter what happens, when he hits that shower the trigger reminds him to stay completely focused on visualizing his critical meeting with Zucor.

Morning triggers strategically placed along the path of your normal routine have proven to be extremely effective. The earlier in the day that you encounter triggers, the better chance they have of establishing stickiness in your mind—and **stickiness is key**. Going out to your car the evening before and placing a trigger note onto your steering wheel is also extremely effective.

Once inside your car, you are in total control of the environment and any distractions. You can choose to turn on the radio and listen to the morning talk shows, or you can decide to focus on visualization or anything else that will improve your performance on this very day. Remember, the choice is yours to make. *Start building your counter-intuitive selling habits today.*

Behavioral Triggers in Action

On this particular morning, Ken discovered the following note on his steering wheel:

> # Call H
> ## ask advice
> ## silence

Stumped by this one? If so, don't worry. Once you understand what it means, you can use it as a template for your own personal triggers.

This was a trigger for Ken to take several actions on his way into the office. Knowing that Helen, his main contact at Zucor, was always in very early in the morning and at her desk organizing her day, he picked up the phone and dialed her number.

When she picked up, Ken wished her a great morning and then got right to the point. "Helen, I just wanted to ask you for any final advice for our meeting later today. What are your thoughts right now?"

With this, Ken stared at the note on his steering wheel. Just as he was tempted to start talking again, he read the word *silence* on his trigger note, so he paused.

Helen started to share a few thoughts. "Ken, I am trying to think back on the last few days since our meeting. The one thing I can share is that this entire project has really gained a lot of visibility lately with the senior team. It's due to the emphasis right now on having the right metrics in place before we start looking at additional cost-cutting measures. The major concern, especially from the heads of the business units, is that they need to feel comfortable that anyone selected for the project understands this, especially the outside vendor. It's metrics first, cost-cutting next. Oh, and they'll want to know who they can talk to at a company where you've assisted in this area before and on a project of this magnitude. Ken, I think that's about it."

Ken knew something about himself. Ken knew he had a habit—a long-ingrained habit—of saying more than he needed to once he posed a question to a customer or prospect. This habit caused a serious problem: it often altered the customer's or prospect's response. He found out the hard way that he sometimes forced customers not to share exactly what was on their mind. Ken wanted to make sure he broke his bad habit once and for all, so his steering wheel trigger note was helping him achieve his goal.

Helen's response would prove extremely valuable later in the day as the meeting at Zucor unfolded. Ken had yet to pull out of his driveway, but he was busy taking notes, and adding these to his file on Zucor. Everything in his file would come into play later in the day.

The Staying Power of Behavioral Triggers

When Ken returned to his car after his midday appointment, he was ready to head out to Zucor for what he believed was the decision-making meeting he had been working toward over the last nine months.

Ken's car key provided the next trigger message. On his key chain, along with his car key, his office key, and his house key, he found two rather large shiny silver paper clips. Ken stared at the paper clips and smiled. These paper clips were his trigger to put everything else away and run through his final visualization (the paper clips triggered him to think "video clip"). He was glad for the reminder, because he was about to pick up the phone to check on a critical order. There would be plenty of time after the visit to Zucor to handle the order and to do anything necessary to get it expedited.

With that, Ken put everything away, turned off his phone and car stereo, and put his briefcase in the backseat. The only things in the front seat with Ken were his Zucor file and the large silver paper clips on his keychain. Those clips triggered his next action—a quiet ride to the Zucor facility and the last run through of the visualization of the meeting. As Ken's confidence grew, he launched into the Zucor movie in his mind.

The Successful Seven: Chapter 8
Action Steps for Mastering the Art of Counter-Intuitive Selling

1. Use trigger notes and trigger objects to remind you of the actions you need to take to turn new behaviors into permanent habits.

2. Place the triggers **along the path** of your normal daily activities.

3. Use **key words and symbolic objects** (e.g., the paper clips) to act as triggers.

4. Avoid the bad habit of thinking **you will remember to act differently without** using strategically placed triggers.

5. At a minimum, **use the exact same triggers for at least 21 consecutive days**.

6. If you find yourself forgetting to use triggers for a day, remember that the **21-day period** of constant trigger use needs to start over.

7. **Thinking will not change habits**; consistent, repeated action will help you to form new behaviors that become new habits.

part two

The Greatest Relationship with the Wrong Decision Maker Gets You Nothing!

The Changing Game of the Decision-Making Process

Changing the game of
selling into a counter-
intuitive game

chapter nine

The Counter-Intuitive Selling Professional Keeps an Ear to the Ground

---

Maintaining a keen sense of the most critical trends and issues facing decision makers is essential. Mentors are a key to this knowledge.

As Ken started his early morning preparation for his key appointments and phone calls later in the day, his mind was busy reviewing all of the issues he was anticipating he would need to cover. He thought back to a meeting he had with one of his key mentors a few months back, and the impact it was now having on his counter-intuitive selling efforts.

For years, Ken had started conversations with customers and prospects by talking about ROI—**R**eturn **O**n **I**nvestment. This turned out to be a very effective technique for getting in the door. Then, Ken could go on to prove to prospects or customers that the solutions he presented offered a compelling ROI equation—meaning that the investment for the solution Ken was selling would create far more financial return within a reasonable period of time, compared to the investment itself.

Once Ken shared this with the rest of his team, they sailed along for quite a while, outsmarting the competition by putting together more compelling ROI calculators and case studies than the competition. In recent months, however, Ken noticed that prospects, and even some of his most coveted customers, were looking for more than a compelling ROI story. They appeared to demand something even more tangible.

Ken realized that, by now, almost every sales professional was coming in and claiming to have a great ROI story, and he suspected that the widespread ROI claims were making some customers and prospects skeptical. The ROI approach still worked with a large number of customers, but Ken was looking for more. He wanted a counter-intuitive solution to help him stay on top of his game.

One of the counter-intuitive selling traits Ken's key mentor, Frank, had instilled in Ken was this: **always maintain a keen sense of the most critical trends and issues facing decision makers—today and tomorrow.** Listen to your customer base to find out what is foremost in their minds and see how your solution plays into solving their most prominent issues. When you can link into their most pressing issues, you create the opportunity to become a valued business partner.

Ken realized one thing early on about Frank, and that was that Frank had the uncanny ability to always boil things down to their simplest form. So, Frank's way of simplifying his advice was to say, **"Find out what problem is keeping that decision maker up at night and then figure out how to solve it.** Better yet, figure out what is going to keep him up tonight and tomorrow night, and get him the solution today. When you do this, you'll have your newest best friend and paying customer!"

As funny as it sounded the first time Ken heard it, it really rang true over the years. In other words, if you need to change and grow your solution to fit your customers' most pressing and immediate needs, then you'd better do it—and do it *quickly*. By doing so, you'll gain their trust and they will do business with you. By not doing so, you leave the door wide open for the competition.

Listening to Your Best Friend and Your Toughest Critic

On Ken's calendar early this morning was his monthly call with Frank. As one of Ken's primary mentors, Frank was always making Ken think differently. Although there were times when Ken would get off the phone with Frank thinking he was at a dead end, their talks usually led to some new thinking and some new ways to attack the market. The answers weren't always easy. These sometimes hard and grueling conversations kept Ken in the game by keeping him in tune with the real decision makers.

Frank was a senior-level decision maker inside a large organization. Although Ken has several mentors who were sales professionals themselves (senior level sales executives), Frank was not a "sales guy," and this was important to Ken. It was critical for Ken to get a nonsales perspective of decision making; he needed a glimpse inside the "C" level of today's organizations without the sale's angle or coloration.

Frank and Ken started their conversation in the usual way. They asked each other about their families and their recent travels. Frank had just come back from India, where his company was in the midst of a multiyear project to set up operations to support much of its customer base around the globe. Frank asked Ken about some of the commitments Ken had shared with him over the past few months.

In addition to helping Ken grow his understanding of business around the globe, Frank was also a personal mentor who helped him challenge and stretch himself. When Ken achieved success, Frank was the first to congratulate him. When Ken slipped, Frank knew how to challenge him to get back up on his feet and back into the race. When Ken needed a swift kick, Frank gave it to him in just the right way. For some reason, Frank knew how to push the right buttons within Ken in order to help him succeed.

This morning, fortunately, Ken was not in need of a swift kick. He was on track with all the commitments that he had made to Frank during their last call. Today, Ken was more interested in hearing what

Frank had to say about what was on the minds of his fellow executives, especially his CEO and the rest of his "C"-level counterparts.

"Ken, I'll tell you what bothers us about this ROI stuff that everybody presents to us these days," Frank started. Ken knew this was going to be one of those calls where Frank took Ken's current approach and proved why it was becoming less effective. As hard as it was at times to hear Frank tear apart his hard work, Ken realized it was the best thing Frank could do for him, and they both knew this was why they were having these conversations.

Frank continued. "ROI projections are all in the future, all based on suppositions and predictions, such as 'each transaction will bring in an additional 20% in revenue' or 'each customer service rep will handle 15 more calls each day.' And it is all based on something that may or may not actually happen. You can't guarantee anything here. It all sounds great, **but it's not concrete**. Think about it, Ken, you can tell somebody like me anything you want to about ROI, and then turn around later and say, 'Well, if you had just done this one more thing, you probably would have reached the ROI we told you about.' Quite frankly, I think the whole conversation is getting a little old."

Ken didn't even have to ask Frank what was discussed in his "C"-level meetings during his trip to India and upon his return. Frank quickly switched gears in his conversation and got right to the point Ken needed to hear.

"Now, let me tell you what we are focused on. We need to understand what our total cost is to move these operations out of the United States. Have we considered everything, and if we have, is the cost really as low as we thought? And, as we look at the technologies we need to do this, will we get a true lower cost of ownership than we had before? Now, this stuff is measurable, and this stuff is real!"

Ken was frantically taking notes as Frank continued. "This concern pertains not only to the relocation going on in India. It applies to any system or change we look at here in the States. We're looking at the same TCO issues; that's what we call this stuff—total cost of ownership issues. The other thing is that we are now always pulling IT into these discussions, and they need to sign off on anything before we move on it. We've seen too many decisions being made around the company that come back to bite us later because we didn't consider the IT implications for integration into our existing systems up front. You know, with technology as pervasive as it is today, we really can't do anything in the company without affecting our systems and IT infrastructure one way or another."

Frank was not an IT-focused executive—not the Frank that Ken knew. It was obvious that Frank had received an education of his own while in India. He was now looking at all of his initiatives through the lens of the IT function, and so were his "C"-level counterparts. This would turn out to be key for Ken as he evolved his strategy and approach moving forward.

Then Frank turned to an area where he had a lot of expertise, having grown up rising through the worlds of human resources (HR) and administration. "We also take a much closer look now at the human component. We ask ourselves if we are able to save heads by moving to a new solution. Might a solution that initially appears to cost us more actually allow us to remove some headcount and therefore lower our labor costs? If so, it is probably the better long-term solution. We're looking at all of these issues before we make any decisions."

What Frank shared next would soon prove to be the most critical piece of information he would leave with Ken from this conversation. "We spend a lot of time capturing all of this and creating potential scenarios. It would be very helpful to us if some of our partners and potential partners would step up to the plate and offer to assist us in all of this groundwork by offering some validation and sharing the experience they have with others in this area."

Reacting Quickly When Trends Change

By now, Ken's brain was spinning—in a great way. Although Frank may have felt that he was simply sharing a recap of his latest month in the ever-changing world of global business, he was providing Ken with the latest glimpse he needed into what was on the top of executives' minds and priority lists. Now Ken needed to figure out how to turn this into an opportunity in his selling efforts.

As he often did when he realized he was on to something significant, Ken became a student. This time, **he became a student of TCO**. The first thing he did when he finished up some urgent client calls was to search the Internet for "total cost of ownership." As always, he was amazed at what he found—white papers, local TCO forums, and more. Ken immediately decided to use two of his I-Team appointments each week to continue his study of TCO and to begin attending one of the monthly TCO forums in his area. He wanted to make sure he started to understand how decision makers really think about TCO and perhaps he could find a true TCO guru to mentor him at one of the forums.

Ken also found a wide variety of definitions for TCO. A lot of the definitions were IT-focused, such as "**total cost of ownership** (TCO) is a model developed to analyze the direct and indirect costs of owning and using hardware and software." He also found some more forward-thinking definitions that mirrored what Frank had shared—the fact that TCO was beginning to be more widely applied to business in general. The statement that Ken liked the most read: "What is TCO? It is how much it really **costs** to own and manage anything in your business."

Ken smiled as he read this definition, and immediately thought to himself, "You know, I think that would be Frank's definition—simple and to the point. Hmm, maybe Frank actually wrote that one. It wouldn't surprise me one bit!"

Ken also kept returning to the last statement Frank shared with him during their most recent conversation: **"If some of our partners would step up to the plate and offer to assist us in all of this groundwork."** From his brief but powerful conversation with Frank that morning, Ken learned several key things that were about to alter his approach. Ken quickly decided that he would immediately put all of this into action as he continued his interaction with "C"-level executives.

Ken was not going to wait for things to change. He was ready to act on the new information. He now understood that total cost of ownership, otherwise known as TCO, is paramount in the mind of senior executives, and it is **something that can be quantified**—easier than ROI can be quantified.

It was time for Ken to change his approach, but only after he put into action what he had learned from Frank in this call.

The Successful Seven: Chapter 9
Action Steps for Mastering the Art of Counter-Intuitive Selling

1. Make sure that you have a "mix of mentors" in your professional sales career that includes a key mentor that comes from a field **other than sales**.

2. Schedule **regular calls and meetings** with your mentors, never going more than a month between phone calls or more than three months between face-to-face meetings with each mentor.

3. Use your mentor base to assist you in staying one step ahead of the competition in knowing **what is foremost on the minds of your customers and prospects** (realize that your customers and prospects are decision makers with profiles similar to those of your mentors).

4. Although return on investment (ROI) remains high in the minds of your customers and prospects, realize that it is hard to quantify and that it remains in the future.

5. **Stay on top of the latest trends and issues** that are critical to decision makers. For example, talk with prospects about how you can impact total cost of ownership (TCO) rather than ROI.

6. Realize that systems (technology) and people (HR) are two of the primary functional areas **where senior-level executives look to impact their business** when looking at solutions.

7. Offer to **assist your customers and prospects in measuring** the value of the solution you bring to the table. For example, offer to prove the advantage of your solution as it pertains to total cost of ownership by working with key members of their team to jointly develop a TCO comparison model.

chapter ten

Gain a Step on the Competition by Being the Game Changer

With your mentors, prospects, and customers as key "change indicators," you have the opportunity to leapfrog the competition. Act *with a sense of urgency* to be the one who changes the prevailing sales conversation.

Ken gained a lot of valuable new information during the conversation with his mentor, Frank, that we shared in our last chapter. Based on all of this information, Ken was getting excited about the potential he saw in the TCO sales conversation.

He also remembered the counter-intuitive definition of insanity: **doing the same things you've always done and expecting different results.** Ken realized that this especially holds true when it comes to the intelligence we gain from our mentors, customers, and prospects. If we do not act on what we learn from our conversations with these sources about key change indicators, we should *not* expect to achieve maximum results in our professional selling career.

Ken definitely knew he needed to change his sales messaging. The ROI bit was getting a little "old" as Frank put it. Ken was trying to decide in what direction to head first. From everything he was reading, he believed he was on the verge of some really compelling new conversations to engage decision makers. However, he was truly challenged with where to start. Should he focus on how his solutions can lower total costs elsewhere? Should he look to see if his higher-priced solution would actually end up costing less than the competition's, given some of the well-hidden but real costs associated with getting his competitor's solution actually up and running? He wondered what his first course of action should be.

Leverage Your Solutions Into New Trends and Issues

It was apparent to Ken that he should begin talking more with his clients and prospects about total cost of ownership, or TCO. Ken needed to look at how his solutions could potentially lower the TCO of other initiatives or systems that his customers own or are about to purchase. Then he remembered the most powerful definition of TCO (the one that he thought could have actually come from Frank) and thought to himself, "**Let's not make this any more complicated than it needs to be**. TCO means how much it *really* costs to own and manage *anything* in your business."

For example, suppose that by combining his solution with a solution already in place inside his customers' operations he could bring cost savings and efficiencies not already built into the existing solution itself. If Ken's automation tool could eliminate steps in the existing process that saved time and resources, it would be a big win for his customers. Even more critically, if Ken's solution could eliminate some of the people currently needed (what his mentors refer to as "human capital"), it could also reduce the potential for human error.

If Ken could develop a TCO comparison showing that the savings gained by combining the two solutions far outweighs the additional investment required, he would be on to something that his customers and prospects would listen to *and* buy into—something that did not exist until Ken created it.

Ken was beginning to formulate another scenario. Perhaps he could come to the table with a solution in which his team took on some administrative and back office work. Ken's company had a great deal of experience and skill in these processes and the available human capital to handle them for hundreds of companies. This scenario would enable Ken's customers to focus on their core business, and it could eliminate their need to carry staff to handle these routine tasks. In reality, he was already doing this for some of his key customers, so why not capitalize on it and use it to create more value?

As Ken thought about this, he started to formulate his value proposition and his opening conversations with prospects and customers about these new opportunities. He believed that his success could be greatly enhanced if he focused his message and solutions on:

- Lowering the total cost of ownership (TCO)—**lowering the real cost to own and manage anything inside his prospects' and customers' businesses.**
- **Combining his new solutions** with already existing solutions to attain a higher level of TCO.
- Allowing his customers and prospects to **focus on their core business** by creating ways for them to offload routine tasks and processes to Ken's team.
- Demonstrating to his customers and prospects that his solutions could **make their existing investments return a higher yield** or payback than they are currently receiving.
- Making it clear he understands the **implications and importance** of working with his customers' and prospects' IT and HR departments to obtain their buy-in and sign-off on the critical intersection that his proposed solutions have to these key segments of their overall business.
- Suggesting to his prospects and customers that he connect with the IT and HR department heads **early on** during initial discussions, even when the customer does not yet make the link in their own minds.

Being an Evangelist When You Are Ahead in the Game

Ken realized that he would need to become an evangelist for the TCO movement. Although there was a lot of recognition and acceptance of TCO validation inside the IT world, it was apparent that it was still a relatively new concept outside of the IT realm. He knew that he needed to be well educated on the TCO subject, so he could share this knowledge with his customers and prospects. TCO made a lot of sense, and it could be very tangible. Results could be measured.

Thinking about this new TCO message reminded Ken of the early days of the ROI approach, when it was just gaining momentum within the sales profession. Although a lot of sales pros talked about it only a few were successful early on in turning it into a real competitive advantage. Ken was determined that he would be one of the first to master TCO as a counter-intuitive selling edge.

Ken was getting more and more excited as he worked all of this through in his mind. Ken remained committed to keeping his I-Team appointments every day—no matter what other issues came up—and using the time to continually refine his selling approach. Those appointments were really beginning to pay off.

He decided to use the next few days of his I-Team appointments to work on incorporating his new thinking into his refined sales messaging. He would solidify the message a little further in his mind, and then revisit it over the next few days. For now, though, he wanted to allow his mind to rest from the intense thinking he was giving to all of this. He needed to put it away for a while, get back to landing more new business, and then revisit the idea to see if it all still made as much sense as it did now. That would be his reality check.

Using Mentors and Customers as a Sounding Board

Ken would also need another—and even more important—reality check for his ideas. Once he solidified in his own mind the foundation of his new messaging and the points he would strive to drive home in his new approach, Ken needed to find an appropriate, real-life sounding board. He needed to have someone verify his thinking and his new messaging.

For this, Ken would make sure to get on his calendar a time to re-connect with Frank for an essential "C"-level 'gut-check.' He wanted to make sure that what he had heard from Frank during their last conversation had translated well into Ken's refocused message and sales approach. In addition, Ken would reach out to a few select prospects and customers—ones that he trusted would give him their absolutely honest feedback and reactions—to share his new message. He would share the reactions and feedback with the rest of his team, and with his manager.

For Ken, there was a side benefit to taking this last step. More often than not, some of the prospects or customers Frank contacts invite him to talk in more detail about his new messaging. That invitation tells Ken that they immediately find enough value in his new message that they want to talk more about it. To Ken, this is the most important validation that he can possibly receive. Knowing from a highly respected customer or prospect that he is on track with his new messaging is a key indicator that he will be successful with his new approach.

When you arrive at Chapter 26 in your journey into the world of counter-intuitive selling, you will see and hear Ken's new messaging in action. For now, however, focus on laying the needed groundwork to make sure your continuing journey into the art of the unexpected is as successful as possible. It's time to take action on what you've learned in this chapter.

The Successful Seven: Chapter 10
Action Steps for Mastering the Art of Counter-Intuitive Selling

1. Do not allow your thinking to **stagnate**.

2. Take what you learn from your mentors and other key contacts and **formulate new and compelling conversation starters** based on what is on the minds of these top-level decision makers—TCO is a great example, but *only* an example, from this chapter.

3. Focus your messaging and conversations on the **latest issues and trends facing decision makers** (as Ken did, for example, with total cost of ownership) letting your prospects and customers know that you understand the concerns that matter most to them.

4. Even if your customer or prospect does not mention it, recommend that **you engage their IT and HR heads early** to understand the concerns of each of these areas and to maximize their involvement early on.

5. Use your I-Team appointments to **continually refine** your sales approach and messaging.

6. Use your key mentors as the **most critical sounding boards** for your new messaging, making sure to validate that you translate what they share with you accurately and in ways that resonate with the "C" level.

7. Reach out to your most trusted prospects and customers to share your new messaging and approach. A **key indicator of the success of your message will be an invitation** from one or more of them to talk more about the topics your new messaging conveys.

chapter eleven

What It All Means to Your Selling Approach and Outcomes

Working your target organizations both deeply and horizontally will ensure success. Establish necessary relationships early to avoid getting blindsided.

Even though it happened to him several years earlier, Ken never forgets the day he realized he lost a huge piece of business—when he was convinced the business was his. He had just left his weekly sales meeting when he got the call from his key contact, the SVP of operations at New Foundry Industrials, one of the country's fastest-growing manufacturers.

When Ken saw the number on his cell phone, he was excited to get the conversation rolling. "I was going to wait until a little later and give you a call. I thought your meeting would go a little longer. How are you, Jim?"

On the other end of the phone was Jim Johnston, the SVP of New Foundry Industrials. As usual, Jim got right down to business. Jim was always focused on the business, and it was probably one of the main reasons for New Foundry's explosive growth. The conversation that was about to unfold also demonstrated just how careful Jim was about every move he made inside New Foundry Industrials.

"Ken, we just left the meeting, and yes, it did end earlier than anticipated—especially earlier than I had anticipated." It was only after Jim shared his next words that Ken began to realize how poorly he had read the situation and how poorly he had executed on a major opportunity.

After all, in the weekly sales meeting he had just left, Ken once again committed the New Foundry deal for the current quarter, and it was now just five weeks from the end of the quarter. Following his plan, Ken had taken his lead from Jim, who was the ultimate decision maker (in addition to being the SVP of operations, Jim also acted as the general manager of all of the manufacturing plants). Ken also had verified that all of the dollars needed for the "green light" on the project were in the budget for the current quarter.

"I feel remiss on my own part," were not the next words that Ken expected to hear from Jim, but it was exactly what he was hearing. "During our meeting today, I was reverifying with all of the functional heads our plans to move forward with the project. It was only at this point that Jack, our head of IT, pointed out that we had never validated with his team that the integration and resources needed from them had been covered as thoroughly as I always expect it to be."

Once Ken heard this, he thought his recovery would be quick, so he responded, "Jim, that's no problem. I will get with Jack and make sure we revisit all of it, in great detail, so that we can move forward as planned. Then I'll circle back to you, as I always do, to make sure we've covered it all. I think we're still in good shape to meet the deadlines we've all established together."

Ken believed everything was back on track until Jim shared what turned out to be the showstopper—one that Ken simply could not recover from this late in the game.

"Ken, I was thinking exactly the same thing, until Jack reminded me that his entire team is committed to the integration of the systems from our acquisition of Mercury Metals. At best, that work will continue until two weeks into the next quarter, and it could go longer. This project is mission critical, as you know, and we cannot pull anyone off of it. As a matter of fact, without this integration completed and up and running effectively, the project with your team cannot even begin."

If Ken had been sitting on his sofa, he would have slipped onto the floor and sat there forever. He had just let the opportunity slip away—at least until next quarter—and with the way business changes by the minute these days, perhaps forever.

From that point forward, Ken never forgot the importance and value of working his target organizations both *deeply* and *horizontally*.

Working Deeply and Horizontally

What does it mean to work "deeply and horizontally"? Let's look at working deeply first. Working deeply means that you do not stop working through decision makers until you are completely convinced that you have reached the real decision maker—the one who will pull the trigger and give the green light for your initiative or project and the funding necessary to move it forward. In Chapters 13 through 16, you'll learn how to identify real decision makers from imposters. For now, realize that getting to the real decision maker is key to your success.

Working horizontally is critical to your success as well, and this is what we'll spend the rest of this chapter discussing. Ken's lost opportunity with New Foundry Industrials is a prime example of what happens when a sales professional fails to work horizontally, to gain information and buy-in from the heads of key functional areas throughout the organization. When you fail to do this, someone surfaces from a functional area, usually the leader of that area, and voices a concern that stalls the opportunity.

If Ken had worked New Foundry Industrials horizontally for this pending deal, he could have either worked with the head of IT to free up resources to keep the project on target to start in the quarter for which he forecast the deal, or he would have known early in the sales cycle that the deal would not close until the following quarter. Either way, Ken could have done what was necessary to save the deal.

The key is to work all of the functional areas that your deal will touch, and work them in parallel, so that when you wind up with the real decision maker ready to execute on the agreement, you know

what the answer will be from the heads of each functional area—a resounding "go."

The functional areas that you want to consider reaching out to as
you work the organization horizontally should include:

- Information technology
- Purchasing (may also be referred to as Procurement)
- Finance
- Human resources
- Training
- Marketing
- Sales

You may find that, depending on the solution you bring to your
customers, different functional areas will be more important as you
work your target organization horizontally.

Following the Unwritten Principle

Ken has learned an important rule of thumb about counter-intuitive selling since his incident with New Foundry Industrials: it's better to touch more areas than you need than to forget to cover a
critical one. You will probably uncover valuable information along
the way, even if in the end the areas with which you establish a
relationship appear to play little or no part in the decision-making
process.

Remember this key unwritten principle of counter-intuitive selling: **it is better to be known within as many parts of your target organizations as possible, than to be an unknown in *any* functional area of
a target organization.**

Let's turn back the hands of time for just a minute (wouldn't you
love to be able to do this for your own lost business!) and imagine
how Ken's discussions might have gone a few years ago if he had

worked the organization horizontally as he does today with every deal in his pipeline.

Ken would have never received the phone call from Jim on that dreadful day, because Ken would have already been working with Jack, the head of IT at New Foundry. He would have fully understood the impact the project brings to Jack's team, and they both would be in full agreement about when the project could launch.

The important conversation would not have happened between Ken and Jim. It would have taken place between Jack and Jim inside New Foundry, and it would have ended there. In their meeting to review the project and give it a green light, Jim would have asked Jack something like, "Jack, are we all set in IT to roll with this?"

If Ken had done all of his counter-intuitive homework and laid the groundwork, Jack would have replied, "Jim, we're in great shape as far as I'm concerned in the IT area. Ken and I have reviewed everything and we're both comfortable with moving ahead on the timeline we've all agreed upon. Let's roll with this and get started."

The good news that came out of Ken's long-remembered lost opportunity from a few years ago is that he learned the importance of working his target organizations horizontally as well as deeply in order to be positioned to win the deal. The even better news is that Ken never makes this mistake now. His counter-intuitive selling skills make sure of that.

The Successful Seven: Chapter 11
Action Steps for Mastering the Art of Counter-Intuitive Selling

1. When you begin to penetrate your target organizations, be sure to work the organizations both **deeply** and **horizontally**.

2. Work *deeply* in order to **get to the *real* decision makers** who will make the actual decisions to move forward with your solutions.

3. Work *horizontally* to be sure to establish a relationship with the key decision maker **in *each* functional area** that will touch your solution in *any way*.

4. Once you establish a relationship with the leader of each of these functional areas, be sure you **fully understand their concerns** regarding your solution and that you both agree on the timelines the actual decision maker wants to follow.

5. Err on the side of establishing relationships with **more functional areas than is necessary** to secure the deal. In the end, having more relationships inside your target organization than you need will only help your efforts.

6. **Never forecast business** in your pipeline as definite business until you have established these horizontal relationships and fully understand their needs relating to your solution.

7. Use the Decision-Maker Rater (discussed in Chapters 13 through 17) **to validate** that you are dealing with a real decision maker and not a "pseudo decision maker."

chapter twelve

How We Make Selling More Complicated Than It Really Needs to Be

---

Without your mentor to help keep you thinking in new ways,
it's easy to slip back into old and detrimental habits.
Your mentor also holds the clues to your best shot at
reaching essential decision makers.

Ken was anxious to get back on the phone with Frank to share where he was headed with his new approach and messaging. There was one thing Ken could always count on from Frank: straightforward feedback without any beating around the bush. As Ken thought about it a little more, he realized that this was probably the reason why Frank continued to be his most important mentor.

Ken called at the time that he had set with Frank's assistant on the calendar, and sure enough, Frank was ready for Ken's call. As always, Frank was upbeat, excited to hear from Ken, and always asking questions.

"Ken, what's going on in your world today? Have you thought more about what I shared in our last conversation? Does it ring true with any of your other mentors and customers? Does it make sense? I've got to tell you that I'm seeing it more and more here."

As the conversation continued, Ken was anxious to hear what Frank would share. As it turns out, another key initiative within Frank's company was stalled based on lack of what both Frank and

Ken were referring to as "horizontal alignment and agreement" on an issue over TCO.

Ken was beginning to feel that he was on to something significant, so he started to share with Frank his thinking on the messaging he was developing. Ken wanted to make sure he hit not only on the issue of TCO, but that he also addressed the horizontal alignment and agreement issue.

"Ken, Ken, Ken," Frank finally said in a very firm voice, "stop, stop, stop."

Ken had worked with Frank as his mentor long enough to know what was coming next, but it took Frank's interruption to get him to stop and think about what was happening.

"Ken, slow down. Keep it simple. You're starting to make it way too complicated! You're even starting to lose me, and I am the one who gave you the idea in the first place! Remember, stick to the basics. You've got the right idea, so don't add what isn't essential for your success!"

Ken heeded Frank's advice, and made sure he stuck to the basics in his new approach. While he was doing this, his very first face-to-face meeting with Frank came back into his mind. It was a meeting in which Frank kept things very simple, *and by doing so drove home a very important lesson.*

Keeping It Simple

Some 20 years ago, after an introductory phone call, Frank had invited Ken to his office. Frank's office overlooked Park Avenue in New York City. Recognizing that Frank was a real decision maker, Ken (who was, at that time, very early in his selling career) was excited to meet with Frank on his turf.

Ken knew that Frank was an early riser. Their introductory conversation took place at about 6:45 one morning, and it was apparent to Ken that Frank had been in the office a while before taking his call. So, when Frank asked Ken, "What time can you get here that morning?" Ken's response was immediate, "Whatever time you want me there."

Later, Frank would explain that Ken's response was one that he should *never* give again in his professional selling career. Ken would never forget the lecture he got from Frank on that one point. "Ken, I don't care if there is not another appointment on your calendar for the next ten years. When you are on the phone with a decision maker, your calendar is always full. Always tell them you have limited time available. Decision makers want to deal with other busy decision makers. It's that simple." Little did Ken know then the power of that lesson, but he knows it now. No matter what, Ken's calendar is always full, especially when he gets on the phone with a decision maker (you'll learn more about this in Chapter 33).

Ken didn't know at the time that Frank was making the most of a learning opportunity by playing into Ken's response to his question. "Great Ken, be here in my office at 6:30 in the morning, and don't be late. We'll have important work to do. See you then."

When the appointed day arrived, Ken did everything to make sure he arrived early. In fact he was 15 minutes early. When he arrived at Frank's office building and the security guard called Frank to let him know of his guest's arrival, he could hear Frank's response to the security guard. "Why good morning, John. So Ken's down there? Great! Show him the way up and I'll see you later today, I am sure. Thanks, John!"

Frank's office was impressive to say the least. Ken noticed one thing right away: the desk was clear of papers. Later, Ken would learn that this was all part of Frank's "clear thinking" strategy. He would always say, "How can you think clearly if your desk is covered with 'stuff'? Clear desk, clear mind. Clear it off, take care of it, touch it once and get it off of your desk for good." This was just one of the many gems that Ken would learn from Frank over the coming years.

They spent most of the morning talking about Frank's guiding principles—the things Frank would later remind Ken about when it came to his new messaging and sales approach. "You know, Ken, we tend to make things far more complicated than they really need to be. It is important that we always keep it simple—simple for us and simple for our current and potential customers. They want to know that it's easy to do business with us."

Since that very first meeting with Frank, Ken came to realize just how difficult it is to continue to keep things simple. In fact, Ken decided that he needed a behavioral trigger to ingrain this thinking into his mind and to make it a habit. With that in mind, Ken created a behavioral trigger card that he keeps inside his Day-Timer. When he opens it during any conversation with a customer, this is the message that greets him:

> **keep it simple/**
> **no unnecessary words**
> **simple = more business**
> **make it easy to do**
> **business with you**

This behavior trigger remains in Ken's Day-Timer, on every page for every day of the year. As a result, he never loses its significance.

Make Contacting Decision Makers Simple

As Ken would learn, everything Frank did had a purpose. "No purpose, no action" was another of Frank's guiding principles that stuck with Ken from that very first day.

At about 6:45 AM in Frank's office, sitting 65 stories above Park Avenue, Frank said, "Ken, come over to the window and look down on the street. Tell me what you see."

Frank looked down on a sea of black limousines and other cars dropping off executive after executive at their offices. Ken was thinking that this must be the second wave of the morning, either that or Frank was unique in that he was always in by 6:30.

A little later, between 8:00 and 8:30, Frank said to Ken, "Now, come stand by the window again, and tell me what you see."

What Ken saw this time was quite different. A sea of yellow taxicabs and busses was dropping off the rest of the workforce. There were also many people on foot, obviously "clock punchers" arriving just before their workday had to begin, and not a minute sooner.

Frank looked at Ken, and posed his defining question: "Now, tell me Ken, when are you going to call to get to the people you need to reach? When will you have access to the people you need to talk to? What will you establish as your critical phone time each day?"

Frank didn't need to say more. His message to Ken was loud and clear: **reach decision makers before the rest of the workforce arrives.** Reach them before their gatekeepers arrive. Reach them when their desks and their minds are clear, and when they are thinking clearly. It was another lesson in simplicity from Frank: keep your calling to decision makers uncomplicated by calling early.

Now Ken needed to distinguish who the real decision makers are, so he can focus on reaching them. He was ready for the next step in this counter-intuitive selling journey.

Before you step in to the next section, it's time to act on the The Successful Seven for the final chapter of this section.

The Successful Seven: Chapter 12
Action Steps for Mastering the Art of Counter-Intuitive Selling

1. Align your **prime phone time** to the key times to reach real decision makers: **before** the rest of the workforce (the "time clock punchers") arrives or **after** the workforce leaves the workplace.

2. Realize that when your mentors question your thinking and actions that they are providing you with **seasoned guidance** on which you should take action.

3. Treat your mentor relationships as **the most important relationships** you establish in your selling career, and work hard to keep these relationships active.

4. Take your mentors' advice seriously and **use behavioral triggers** to drive behavior changes that turn your mentors' advice and guidance into new habits.

5. Remember that a key to your success lies in **making it easy** for your prospects and customers to do business with you.

6. Look for ways to **reward your mentors** for the time and invaluable advice and guidance they provide to you. Introduce them to your other mentors, send business their way, and invite them to events that you know will be beneficial to their business.

7. Compare the advice you receive from each of your mentors to **uncover trends** in their combined advice and guidance, and act on these trends with a sense of urgency.

Find Out "Who's Who" with the Decision-Maker Rater

Sizing up your contacts
through one of the most
powerful selling tools
ever created

chapter thirteen

With Whom Are You Really Dealing?

In order to truly master the art of the unexpected, counter-intuitive selling professionals use the Decision-Maker Rater *quickly size up their contacts and relationships.*

As Ken headed back to the office for the weekly sales meeting, he was quite excited to share the revelations he had experienced about a major target prospect. He was making good progress in getting to G.U.I.D.O. and he was excited about his newly found H.A.N.K. in the legal department.

As it turns out, the new H.A.N.K. was a real up-and-coming star in the company, and the tip-off he passed along from a salesperson inside the company was the best little piece of counter-intuitive intelligence Ken had received in months. Ken was thankful that he had not spent any more time attempting to establish a relationship with the N.E.R.D.—the one that he initially thought was more of a H.E.R.B. or perhaps even a G.U.I.D.O.-in-training. As it turned out, the N.E.R.D. was really much more of a G.U.I.D.O. wannabe.

Are you sitting there scratching your head, wondering: What is all of this G.U.I.D.O. stuff? Who are H.A.N.K. and H.E.R.B? What on earth is a N.E.R.D?"

What is a G.U.I.D.O.-in-training or a G.U.I.D.O. wannabe? And, most importantly, what does all of this have to do with *my* selling career?

My best advice to you is fasten your seat belt, and hold on for the ride. This is the ride that is *guaranteed* to change your selling career forever.

Meet the Decision-Maker Rater Characters

The number one mistake that most salespeople make today is **misidentifying decision makers.**

What do I mean by this?

Put in the simplest terms possible, most salespeople convince themselves that they are dealing with a decision maker, only to find out when it is *too late* that the individual they are dealing with **does not, will not,** and **cannot** make the decision. Instead, another person in the organization actually makes the decision, and more often than not, the business slips away—usually to your number one competitor (you'll read more about this in the next chapter).

Does this sound familiar? Are we hitting a little too close to home? Are you looking for a way to get out of this cyclical pattern, and to get into a world where you can be guaranteed that you are working with the real decision maker?

The Decision-Maker Rater is the tool that will help you.

The Players of the Decision-Maker Rater

In the next few chapters, you'll get to know the major players of the Decision-Maker Rater in greater detail. For now, the following brief descriptions will make it easy to separate all **real and pseudo decision makers** into four main categories:

1. *N.E.R.D.* A pseudo decision maker who can never, and will never, make a decision—a **N**ever-**E**nding **R**evolving **D**oor.
2. *H.E.R.B.* Someone who will become a new best friend as he or she goes about **H**elping (you) **E**arn **R**espect and **B**ucks while he or she either makes the decision to do business with you or influences this decision.
3. *H.A.N.K.* Another new best friend that assists you by **H**elping (you) **A**cquire **N**ew **K**nowledge that enables you to get to the real decision maker and land the deal.

4. ***G.U.I.D.O.*** The real deal! The **G**enuine **U**pper **I**ncome **D**ele-gating **O**fficial who pulls the trigger on the buying decision (or gives the final approval "nod"), often on the advice of H.A.N.K. and/or H.E.R.B.

There is a powerful counter-intuitive saying: remember, G.U.I.D.O. leads to *the gold* and N.E.R.D. leads you *absolutely nowhere*, so it's time to **get to G.U.I.D.O!**

Using these acronyms and fictitious (but ever so real) characters to quickly size up and categorize your contacts within each prospect and customer is an invaluable boost to your sales performance. It also makes conversations with your sales team about account strategy much shorter. Everyone talks a common language about contacts and major players within accounts.

There is an interesting point about the value of H.A.N.K. and H.E.R.B. Although G.U.I.D.O. is the ultimate prize, H.A.N.K. and H.E.R.B. many times provide the key and the "gateway" to G.U.I.D.O.

The Decision-Maker Rater in Action

The day was about to get a lot more interesting for Ken and the rest of his sales team. Today was the day for the semiannual joint sales meeting with the other East Coast team. The other team was not yet using the Decision-Maker Rater, so Ken knew it would be interesting to see how the two teams interacted during the forecast and pipeline portion of the meeting. The groups were competitive enough as it was, but now Ken and his team had an edge that they were ready to share with the other team that would enable their pipeline reviews to become more accurate and succinct.

The two forecast and pipeline reviews were radically different in several ways. Ken's team completed its review in one-third the time of the other team. Decision makers were clearly identified, and strate-gies were laid out and described in terms of the number of **H.A.N.K.s** and **H.E.R.B.s** involved, along with initiatives underway to neutralize

N.E.R.D.s. True **G.U.I.D.O.s** were known in each and every opportunity, along with the steps needed to secure the buying decision.

When the other team delivered its forecast and pipeline review, it was needlessly long, with extended dialog that the team members were beginning to realize could easily be replaced by defining key contacts as **H.A.N.K.**, **H.E.R.B.**, **N.E.R.D.**, and **G.U.I.D.O.** The other team's strategies were not clear, or at least these weren't as clearly articulated as those outlined by Ken's team. Keith, a member of the other region's sales team, was in the middle of his forecast review when Ken yelled out, "Hey Keith, you've been forecasting that deal for the past six months. The guy you are dealing with sounds like a N.E.R.D. When are you going to give it up and either find a H.A.N.K. or a H.E.R.B. to lead you to the real business, or move on?"

After taking three times as long to deliver its review, the other team was ready to launch into a training session on the Decision-Maker Rater. Ken and his team were glad to help them get over the learning hump so they could fully utilize the Decision-Maker Rater.

The Power of the Decision-Maker Rater

Are you wondering just how useful the Decision-Maker Rater really can be? Let's say you are moving through the sales cycle with what appears to be a great opportunity. Your contact is telling you all the right things and indicating that he or she is the one who makes the decision. Every week in your sales meeting you forecast this "deal," letting your sales manager know that it looks solid and that you are dealing with the decision maker.

Then one day everything changes. You get the dreaded phone call. Your contact tells you that the decision has been made to award the business to one of your competitors, and that she actually just learned about it right before the call.

This is one of the most dreaded and yet common occurrences in sales today—one that you are about to put an end to once and for all, thanks to the Decision-Maker Rater and your four new best friends.

What you learn in the next few chapters will enable you with the counter-intuitive intelligence you need to make sure you've received the last of these dreaded phone calls from a prospect or customer.

But first, be sure to take time to act on The Successful Seven from this chapter.

The Successful Seven: Chapter 13
Action Steps for Mastering the Art of Counter-Intuitive Selling

1. Commit to **mastering the next four chapters** of this book.

2. Complete the exercises in each of the next four chapters—one at a time—and **do not move on to the next chapter until** all exercises in each chapter are completed.

3. As you read each chapter, **find a current prospect** in which the individual you are dealing with is the character discussed in the chapter. Use this prospect as the real-life example for the chapter.

4. Understand that a **H.A.N.K.** or a **H.E.R.B.** within your key customer and prospect organizations **can be as valuable as G.U.I.D.O.** (We'll cover this in more detail in the next few chapters. For now, keep this thought fresh in your mind as we continue.)

5. Embrace the characters within the Decision-Maker Rater as a common language that your sales team will now use to discuss all opportunities in the pipeline.

6. As you learn each of the characters within the Decision-Maker Rater, begin to identify **each contact within your customer and prospect organizations** as a G.U.I.D.O., H.A.N.K., H.E.R.B., or N.E.R.D.

7. Use the language of the Decision-Maker Rater as **a tool to shorten** sales meetings, pipeline reviews, and account strategy discussions.

chapter fourteen

N.E.R.D.s Will Lead You to the "Dead End Zone" of Sales

You may be there already and not even know it, until you understand the never-ending revolving door and his traits.

Ken had been dealing with this prospect, Abacus Financial, for quite some time. At every forecast review Ken was upbeat, convinced of his progress and the size of the opportunity. He was certain it was real, having mapped it with his opportunity-profiling tool, tracing the decision-making steps, and covering most of the other bases required by his sales manager.

Ken's contact even confirmed that he was the decision maker and that no one else needed to be involved for things to move forward. It all added up quite nicely and sounded like a solid opportunity when Ken reviewed it in the weekly team calls, except for one telltale sign and **danger signal: there was no movement in the sales cycle**. Week after week, month after month, things appeared to be moving forward, but there was no real progress. There was plenty of "activity" with the account, of course; lots of meetings, discussions, and "to dos" for Ken and members of the support team. You could easily look at the account and feel like things were moving along.

But the lack of real progress concerned Ken for some very good reasons. He was beginning to **notice a pattern** with a number of his deals. In each of them, even though Ken "felt" like he was dealing with the right individual and the decision maker, in the end, he would eventually find out from his key contact (at the time he didn't realize these were all never-ending revolving doors, or N.E.R.D.s) that the business had gone elsewhere. In most of these situations, Ken's contact would apologize to him, telling him he or she was not sure how or why this happened. The two would commiserate together, rationalize their way through the disaster, and begin talking about doing business together in the future.

Is any of this starting to sound familiar?

There was quite an interesting facet to all of this, as Ken found out when he started to really push his "pseudo decision makers"—his N.E.R.D.s—to learn what was really going wrong. In answer to his questions, Ken began to hear things like, "Well, when it went up for review…" or "When it went for approval to my boss…." The worst explanation from a N.E.R.D. that Ken heard, the one that went right to his gut, was, **"The decision happened, and I was not even aware of it."**

He was puzzled, and when he questioned the N.E.R.D.s even further, they all explained, in a matter-of-fact way, that "of course" someone else had to approve or review the deal. This information contradicted earlier conversations with his contacts, and sometimes their new conversations started to verge on confrontation. Ken wanted all of it to stop.

The light bulb went off in Ken's head. His key contacts were convinced, in their minds, that they were the decision makers. In their line of thinking, needing someone else's "review" or "approval" did not mean that someone else is making the decision. In reality, we know that this "review" or "approval" is real and the final step of the decision-making process. Many of Ken's contacts truly fit the N.E.R.D. profile.

Ken had had enough, and he was ready to take action to stop this pattern. He was ready to change his habits. To get started, he needed to enter the world and the mind of the **N.E.R.D.**

Understanding the Mind of a N.E.R.D.

We have all dealt with the type of character we call N.E.R.D. (probably many of them) in our sales career. We also have all been fooled by one of them, either temporarily or for an extended time.

Are you ready to get into the mind of N.E.R.D.s? If you are, enter it only after you make a career-changing commitment to yourself. Commit that you are entering it only to understand it and to learn how to leave it behind once and for all. **Commit to yourself now to never get trapped by N.E.R.D.s again in your sales career.** Never let a N.E.R.D. control a deal for you or stop you from getting the real business that is on the table!

N.E.R.D. deals are those that stay in our pipeline forever, with little movement up in the sales process. We really believe the N.E.R.D. At times, we think we are making progress. We even try to convince our boss that the deal is "eminent." Even worse, we look at our sales pipeline and it looks full. We gain a false sense of confidence that we will hit our numbers and beat our quota!

Welcome to the world of N.E.R.D.s.

There are very valid reasons why we start to believe a N.E.R.D. A N.E.R.D. can be very believable. He will try his best to convince you that he makes the decision—he'll even make sure to steer you away from the *real* decision makers. In fact, he'll make it clear that it is not a good idea for you to try to deal with anyone else in the organization.

Research gathered during 20 years of delivering the sales training program *MindsetMARKETING: A proven system to sell to high level decision makers*™ has provided a succinct profile of a N.E.R.D. and points to the warning signs you should watch for in identifying these individuals. See for yourself if reviewing the N.E.R.D. profile sets off an alarm in your mind about any deals currently in your sales forecast.

Profile: N.E.R.D. (Never-Ending Revolving Door)

Personality Traits: Detail-oriented, analytical, dry, tunnel vision, cautious, security-oriented, risk-adverse, loyal, technical, in control of empire, protective, devil's advocate, price-driven, inflated ego/ power trip, conservative.

How They Think:

"How does this fit my needs?"

"How is this going to change my job?"

"How does this give me more power?"

Like to Talk About: Their projects; facts, figures, features, functions; details, details, details; the elongated process to get deals done in their company.

Their Success Stories: How they solved a problem; a raise; industry associations; their gain at someone else's expense, their expertise; no problems, no risks, keeping the status quo; their promotion, someone else's demise.

What They Tell You: The decision is theirs to make; no one else needs to be involved; going over their head is not a good idea; other people who want to be involved are jerks.

Warning Sign Alert: Any one of the above traits/characteristics alone may not be cause for a high level of concern. Some of these characteristics may seem at odds with each other; however, the combinations are what become lethal to your sales career. When the warning signs begin to add up and multiply, it's time to retreat and restrategize!

If the alarms are starting to sound about a number of deals in your pipeline, then now is the time to act. You've already taken the first critical step—a step some of the best sales professionals fail to take—by realizing that you've got some N.E.R.D.s to deal with before you move forward. With this critical **step of awareness**—awareness of the presence of the N.E.R.D.s and that you must change your habits—you are on the right track to becoming a counter-intuitive selling success.

The good news is that there are proven strategies and techniques that will assist you in getting beyond the N.E.R.D.s and out of the "dead end zone" of selling. This is what counter-intuitive selling is all about.

Getting Past the N.E.R.D.

It all started for Ken when he realized that his major contact within another account, Farris Wheeler, was indeed a N.E.R.D. Although Ken had a great relationship with this N.E.R.D., the warning bells were sounding in his brain—and sounding loudly!

Ken realized that he had a major decision to make: continue this "nice and comfortable" relationship with the N.E.R.D. and continue to get *no business* from the account, or look for new contacts and begin to wean himself from the N.E.R.D.

In the end, it was an easy decision for Ken, but only after he **emotionally detached himself** from his relationship with the N.E.R.D. This is another key piece of counter-intuitive selling that you must master if you want to achieve the success that is within your reach.

A main reason that many professional salespeople fail to gain the business within their reach is the **emotional attachment they develop with their contacts**. Many times, those contacts are N.E.R.D.s. The emotional attachment produces what we in the world of counter-intuitive selling refer to as a "**blind spot.**"

When we have a blind spot caused by our personal relationship with a N.E.R.D., we cannot see the damage we are doing to our potential to do business with the prospect. We start to worry about situations that could occur in the future. "What if I upset N.E.R.D. by going to someone else?" or "The N.E.R.D. has made it clear several times that I should not talk to other departments or attempt to talk to his boss," are the thoughts that fill our mind.

If this sounds all too familiar to you, then it is time to face the facts about N.E.R.D.s: you will not get anywhere by continuing this relationship the way it is today.

Before you get too depressed about the dead ends you are facing in accounts in which a N.E.R.D. is one of your key contacts, we have some good news. The two new characters you are about to meet, H.A.N.K. and H.E.R.B., will become your new best friends inside these same prospects and customers. The H.A.N.K.s and H.E.R.B.s you meet will lead you to even more business. Even better, they are easier to deal with than N.E.R.D.s, they will have your interests in mind (you'll find out why in the next chapter), and they will speed the process along rather than slowing it down—the way N.E.R.D.s typically do.

Now let's continue on our path to mastering counter-intuitive selling by putting the following action steps into practice right now. Remember, **changing your sales habits and becoming truly counter-intuitive** in your actions and results requires practice and a plan. Before you head into the next chapter, find time to take action in order to make permanent changes in your selling career. This is a great way to utilize your I-Team appointment time this week.

Remember, identifying N.E.R.D.s is one of the most critical steps in your journey toward mastering the art of the unexpected, so do not overlook the opportunity to get intimately familiar with the profile and characteristics of N.E.R.D. Read and review this chapter *at least twice* before you move on to the next chapter, and come back and refer to this chapter often.

Your sales success depends upon it.

The Successful Seven: Chapter 14
Action Steps for Mastering the Art of Counter-Intuitive Selling

1. **Emotionally detach yourself** from your relationships with N.E.R.D.s to remove "**blind spots**" that prevent progress toward landing business within target prospects and customers.

2. **Match each of your main contacts** for every deal in your current pipeline against the N.E.R.D. profile.

3. Create a **"take action" list of deals** in instances where the N.E.R.D. profile matches the identity of your main contact.

4. Review the last three to six months of activity in each of these accounts to **validate that your main contact fits the N.E.R.D. profile** (look for stalled activity or "busy work" with no real progress in the sales cycle).

5. When you verify that a main contact is a N.E.R.D., target this account for an **"Escape the N.E.R.D." action plan**.

6. Immediately **alert your sales manager** to this list of deals, and enlist his or her assistance to avoid losing the business.

7. Keep this target "Escape the N.E.R.D." account list **in hand** as you read the next two chapters and begin to build your escape plan.

chapter fifteen

H.A.N.K.s and H.E.R.B.s Are Your Best Sources of Counter-Intuitive Intelligence

More important than occasionally finding a H.A.N.K. or a
H.E.R.B. who actually *makes the decision*
you will learn everything you need to know from them.

Ken was quite pleased and confident with the way that things were shaping up for him inside Farris Wheeler, Inc. Over the past few months he had gained a thorough understanding of the organization's key objectives for the next 18 months and he had also gained an understanding of "who's who" when it comes to the decision-making process.

There was another very good reason why Ken was feeling confident about the opportunity—an opportunity to strike it big with Farris Wheeler. During these last few months Ken had been invited to participate in a number of key committee meetings inside Farris Wheeler. At these meetings, he had the opportunity to hear about the issues firsthand, and he also met a number of important individuals he otherwise would have never met. In fact, he would have never known of their existence or their significance. These contacts would prove to be key as things progressed.

Just a few months earlier, Ken felt he was making no progress at all with Farris Wheeler, although he was certain that the account offered significant opportunity. There had been meetings—plenty of them, and responses to requests for proposals (RFPs)—but in the end, there had been no business.

This all began changing quickly when Ken had decided to move beyond his N.E.R.D. within Farris Wheeler, and look for his two new best friends, H.E.R.B. and H.A.N.K.

Meeting H.E.R.B.—*H*elping (You) *E*arn *R*espect and *B*ucks

When you realize a contact fits the H.E.R.B. profile, you want to do everything possible to establish a significant and long-lasting relationship. H.E.R.B.s are upbeat and are viewed in the organization as people who get things done. They also are in the know, because they "have G.U.I.D.O.'s ear." They could be on their way, in fact, to becoming a G.U.I.D.O. (You'll learn more about G.U.I.D.O. in our next chapter).

H.E.R.B. is critical to your success in counter-intuitive selling. More importantly, **overlooking H.E.R.B. will create another blind spot for you**—one that will let business slip into the hands of the competition. One of your worst enemies can be a H.E.R.B. that is entrenched within your competition, so make sure this never happens to you! Use the following profile to identify the H.E.R.B.s among your contacts.

Profile: H.E.R.B. (Helping Earn Respect and Bucks)

Personality Traits: Confident, risk taker, consensus builder, "big picture" thinker, team player, always learning, involved, and in-the-know.

How They Think:

> "How does this help the company?"

> "How can I accelerate progress?"

> "Does this fit with G.U.I.D.O.'s top initiatives?"

> "Will this help my team achieve its objectives?"

Like to Talk About: Their success, their team, their progress within the organization; their contacts, the influence they can have on others, their willingness to stick their neck out for something they believe; their relationship with G.U.I.D.O.

Their Success Stories: Key initiatives they lead, their relationships with G.U.I.D.O.s; their rise within the organization; their recognition within the industry; their ability to get results for the organization; their "inside information" that allows them to know "the real story."

What They Tell You: How you need to approach an opportunity to win; what is most important to their organization; how to get visibility with G.U.I.D.O.; who else you need to get to know; the real organizational chart versus the "published one."

How to Find H.E.R.B.: Ask around for the names of "movers and shakers"; look for trends in the names of others that a N.E.R.D. either fears or speaks negatively about. These individuals could very well be a H.E.R.B.; ask a salesperson within your target customer or prospect.

KEY LEVERAGE POINT: If what you bring to the table is valuable to his company, a H.E.R.B. will champion your efforts and become your personal coach to get the business.

And Don't Forget H.A.N.K.—*H*elping (You) *A*cquire *N*ew *K*nowledge)

H.A.N.K. can prove to be key when you need to learn more details and when you need to find an ally within your target prospect or customer. Together, H.A.N.K. and H.E.R.B. are the combination that can lead you to a lot of new business and—directly or indirectly—to G.U.I.D.O.

As you uncover the H.A.N.K.s within your target prospect and customer accounts, you may not feel that these individuals are as dynamic or as visible as H.E.R.B.s, which is why you may need to have a H.E.R.B. lead you to a H.A.N.K.

Here's the profile of a H.A.N.K. Notice both the similarities to and the differences from a H.E.R.B.

Profile: H.A.N.K. (Helping Acquire New Knowledge)

Personality Traits: Expert within his/her domain; project/timeline-oriented; more detail-oriented than a H.E.R.B.; more focused on their domain area versus complete big picture (although aware of the big picture); both results- and task-oriented

How They Think:
   "How can my team improve to help the company?"
   "What different thinking can help us get better results?"
   "How do I build a case to get G.U.I.D.O.'s buy-in?"

Like to Talk About: Their contributions and their team; more details than a H.E.R.B. discusses; improving results; their dependency on the ability of others to deliver; how decisions in other areas affect their area (always positive about the eventual outcome).

Their Success Stories: Delivering on time; improvements to processes; cross-functional cooperation; creating "wins" for G.U.I.D.O.; using their expertise and experience to create success.

What They Tell You: Important details that you might otherwise overlook or not have access to; who really makes decisions and how to influence these decisions; validation of a H.E.R.B.'s ability to influence decisions; what *not* to do if you really want the business.

How to Find H.A.N.K.: A H.E.R.B. often leads you to a H.A.N.K. In addition, look for functional heads in key areas; forward-thinking heads of traditionally conservative functional areas (human resources, purchasing/procurement); look for leaders of key initiatives that are not necessarily at the highest level of the organizational structure (for example, a project manager suddenly in charge of a key company initiative).

KEY LEVERAGE POINT: If a H.A.N.K. believes that what you bring to the table will help the efforts of his team and accomplish his key objectives, he will bring your solution to the table for consideration and he will personally endorse it.

Making Use of H.A.N.K.s and H.E.R.B.s

Inside Farris Wheeler, Ken had gained the trust and friendship of both a key H.E.R.B. and a key H.A.N.K., and he was on his way to a meeting with another H.E.R.B. This H.E.R.B. surfaced during a meeting at Farris Wheeler last week, and Ken received an introduction from his original H.E.R.B. H.E.R.B #1 described H.E.R.B. #2 as "another up and coming member of the team that you need to know," adding, "At times, G.U.I.D.O. listens to him even more than he listens to me."

H.A.N.K. was heading up a key transformation initiative inside manufacturing. It was a pet project of G.U.I.D.O.'s, so stakes were high and H.A.N.K. was keeping things on track and progressing in the right direction. Ken had met H.A.N.K. through his first H.E.R.B., and now he was about to meet H.E.R.B. #2.

Ken had decided he needed to meet his first H.E.R.B. after compiling all of his notes from several months of meetings inside Farris Wheeler That H.E.R.B.'s name was coming up again and again in meetings; he seemed to be in the thick of things, and was always talked about as someone who was "making an impact" and "getting things done."

After a meeting a few months ago at the Farris Wheeler corporate headquarters, Ken decided to walk the long way through the building rather than quickly exit to the parking lot. When he did this, he was able to walk through the sales and customer service areas, which were always buzzing with action. Because Ken had done this on numerous occasions after meetings, a number of the people that worked in sales recognized him.

One of the women that Ken always stopped to talk with was just returning from the cafeteria. As they walked together down the hallway, Ken struck up a conversation with her, and then mentioned H.E.R.B., waiting for her reaction. When she responded, Ken knew he had to get to know H.E.R.B. "H.E.R.B. is really making a difference and getting things done that really need to get done. I think it won't be long before he is at the VP level and working for G.U.I.D.O." Then

Ken went for the most important next step, and asked her advice on getting to see H.E.R.B.

"Go by his office on your way out," she responded. "Let me show you where he sits."

With that, Ken received a quick introduction. H.E.R.B. agreed to have lunch the following week when Ken was back in the area. Ken knew he was on to something big, and it was all the result of taking advantage of the opportunity to just wander around the building. Ken had learned that "wandering around time" was key to success in counter-intuitive selling.

The next time he was in the building, he was going to make sure he "wandered by" G.U.I.D.O.'s office with H.E.R.B. walking right beside him.

Use your relationships with both H.A.N.K.s and H.E.R.B.s in the same way Ken does—to increase your visibility and awareness with G.U.I.D.O.s while you are, at the same time, increasing your knowledge of your key prospect. Wander around. Be visible. Appear connected. Be counter-intuitive!

Now, take a moment to review The Successful Seven for this chapter.

The Successful Seven: Chapter 15
Action Steps for Mastering the Art of Counter-Intuitive Selling

---

1. Use the profiles of H.E.R.B.s and H.A.N.K.s to **get to know their personality traits** and to identify them among your target prospects and customers.

2. **Search out** H.E.R.B.s and H.A.N.K.s within both your target prospects and customers.

3. **Change your old habits immediately** by focusing on building relationships with H.E.R.B.s and H.A.N.K.s rather than N.E.R.D.s.

4. Realize that both H.E.R.B.s and H.A.N.K.s **can be threatening to N.E.R.D.s**, so do not expect a N.E.R.D. to respect any H.E.R.B. or H.A.N.K.

5. Review all of your past meeting notes and contacts within your target prospects and customers to **begin to identify** your first H.E.R.B. and H.A.N.K. candidates.

6. Formulate a game plan to utilize **counter-intuitive "wander around" time** inside your target prospect and customer locations and corporate headquarters. Use this time to **talk with as many individuals as possible** in your efforts to "scout out" your next H.A.N.K. and/or H.E.R.B.

7. Remember that H.E.R.B.s and H.A.N.K.s are **your gateways to G.U.I.D.O.s**—both *directly* and *indirectly*.

chapter sixteen

Visibility with and Acceptance by G.U.I.D.O. Is the Prize at the End of the Journey

---

Creating awareness of who you are and what you bring to the table is a key counter-intuitive goal. G.U.I.D.O needs to know—directly or indirectly.

As Ken was getting ready to depart the Farris Wheeler headquarters, he was again walking with H.E.R.B. through the executive area—another convenient "wandering around" trick Ken had learned during his journey into counter-intuitive selling.

As they passed G.U.I.D.O.'s office and his executive assistant, Ken looked over and said, "Good morning, Susan, how are you today?" Susan looked at Ken and said, "I'm doing well. How about you?"

Perhaps it was the element of surprise or the fact that Susan did not want to appear to not know Ken when he obviously knew her. Truth be known, this was the first time Ken had ever seen Susan. However, from where her desk was situated in relation to G.U.I.D.O.'s office and also her nameplate, Ken had all the ammunition he needed.

H.E.R.B. looked over at Ken and then at Susan. It was apparent he also assumed that Ken and Susan, somehow or someway, knew each other before today. H.E.R.B.'s next comment convinced Ken that his counter-intuitive actions were really beginning to pay off.

"G.U.I.D.O. asked me the other day how my discussions with you were progressing, and if I saw value in your recommendations," H.E.R.B. said quietly to Ken.

"How did you respond to him?" Ken asked.

"The way I usually do," H.E.R.B. responded with a smile. "I said, 'Why else would I be meeting with him again?'"

It was Ken who was now smiling—only he was just smiling to himself, making sure his sense of satisfaction was not overly noticeable to H.E.R.B. In reality, Ken had not yet met G.U.I.D.O. He was not, however, about to let H.E.R.B. know this—unless of course, H.E.R.B. asked Ken directly.

If there was one thing Ken learned early on from his mentors during his journey into counter-intuitive selling it was this: **honesty and integrity above all else.** As Frank once said, "Ken, there is one thing that no one can take away from you—*your integrity.* You are the only one that can ever diminish it, and don't ever even think of doing it!"

Ken realized why G.U.I.D.O., whom Ken had not yet met, was asking H.E.R.B. questions about him. It was all thanks to Ken's counter-intuitive *PowerNotes,* a very powerful tool that we'll explore in Chapter 32. Right now, let's learn more about G.U.I.D.O.

Meeting G.U.I.D.O.–*G*enuine *U*pper *I*ncome *D*elegating *O*fficial

There are some very key reasons why a G.U.I.D.O. is a G.U.I.D.O. and why he has achieved the success that he has in his career. A G.U.I.D.O. is obviously an accomplished leader, and he has many of the characteristics of a great leader. **But always remember that the "D" in G.U.I.D.O. stands for delegating.** A G.U.I.D.O. did not get to where he is without learning to successfully execute on the art of delegation. He will not remain in his position as a G.U.I.D.O. without continuing to execute on the art of delegation.

As sales professionals, especially before we enter the world of counter-intuitive selling, we often overlook the "D" element of a G.U.I.D.O.'s position, and we even try to fight it. When you enter the world of counter-intuitive selling, it is time to stop fighting the "D" element. It is time to make it work for you.

Getting to G.U.I.D.O.

Frank, Ken's mentor, used to quiz Ken as part of their early mentoring sessions. One day, Frank said to Ken, "How high do you call when you first try to make contact with a new target prospect?"

Back then Ken was a typical hot shot, up-and-coming sales professional, so he fired back immediately to Frank, "As high as possible, of course! Why do you ask?"

"Come on Ken, use that brain of yours!" Frank fired back. "G.U.I.D.O. pays a lot of great people on his team a lot of money just so he can delegate responsibility and decisions to them. So be careful! You're not going to earn the respect of G.U.I.D.O. if you do not recognize this and realize who you need to call on to get decisions."

Then Frank said something profound. "This doesn't mean that you don't involve G.U.I.D.O. and that you don't keep him 'in the know' about your efforts and conversations with his people. It just means you have to be smart about how and when you try to get to G.U.I.D.O. directly. He'll be involved and informed, believe me. That's his job. Just remember, he pays others to make decisions and get the job done. The bigger the organization that G.U.I.D.O leads, the more you need to practice this art."

Ever since that conversation with Frank, Ken has learned to leverage his visibility with and access to G.U.I.D.O.s. Many times, Ken learns from H.E.R.B.s and H.A.N.K.s when it is the right time to come **face to face** with G.U.I.D.O. At other times, Ken uses his relationship with H.E.R.B.s to **indirectly** get to G.U.I.D.O.s. Regardless of which road Ken takes, he is sure of one point thanks to his counter-intuitive selling sense: G.U.I.D.O. is well aware of Ken and the impact Ken brings to the table.

The profile of G.U.I.D.O. lets us know, as counter-intuitive selling professionals, how we need to interact with G.U.I.D.O.s, as well as how to leverage visibility with G.U.I.D.O.s. Now, take a look at the G.U.I.D.O. profile, so you can learn to recognize him among your current and future contacts.

Profile: G.U.I.D.O. (Genuine Upper Income Delegating Official)

Personality Traits: Power, authority, ego, motivation, open-minded, optimistic, forward-thinking, decisive, strategic planner, risk taker, proactive, hard to reach, delegator, results-oriented, charismatic, in charge, takes ownership.

How They Think:

"How does this increase stakeholder value?"

"Does this get us to our long-term goals?"

"Does this solve the issues that keep me up at night?"

"Will this give us a better position in the marketplace?"

"Will this help me keep my position as G.U.I.D.O?"

Like to Talk About: Their success, their team, their company, circles of influence, community involvement, quality of products/services, leading the industry, key customers, level of success, their peers, growing the organization, new ideas, thinking about things differently.

Their Success Stories: Increasing market share, improving stakeholder value, leading through change, industry recognition for the organization, vision, growth, up-and-coming talent in the organization, growing people and growing the organization.

What They Tell You: What they need; impact to the business of their decisions; who to talk to in order to gain needed support; what the end goal is; who not to bother with inside their organization; what to do next to stay on their radar screen and under consideration.

How To Find G.U.I.D.O.: Easiest person to identify through Web site, annual report, shareholder information; when all else fails—ASK!

KEY LEVERAGE POINT: Prove you have the best solution to his or her most pressing problems and most important initiatives, and G.U.I.D.O. will listen or make sure others in the organization listen to you.

When G.U.I.D.O. Reaches Out to You

When you truly begin to master the art of the unexpected, you will begin to see and feel the power of establishing both indirect and direct relationships with G.U.I.D.O.s. Ken realized this one day as he headed back to his car after an early morning breakfast with a H.E.R.B. from one of his target prospects.

As he reached for his cell phone, Ken saw that he had four messages waiting. The first message proved to be the most interesting. A smile grew on Ken's face as he listened to it:

"Hi Ken, my name is Jean Mitchell. I'm the executive assistant to John Roberts, the CEO of Landworks Metals. I don't think we've spoken before, but John asked me to call you to get time set on your schedule to come in and talk with him. John had a meeting yesterday with Jim Sylvester and, based on something they discussed, John asked me to get you on his calendar. You can return my call at 555-274-8301. Thank you."

It was a most interesting message to receive. Ken was doing business with Jim Sylvester's organization—some very significant business—but he had never directly met Jim. He had only "met" him through his PowerNotes to Jim, as Jim is the head G.U.I.D.O. at his company. This provided further validation to Ken that counter-intuitive selling was really beginning to pay big dividends.

Though Landworks Metals was on Ken's high-potential prospect list, it was an account that he had not yet directly started to penetrate. Now, based on his counter-intuitive selling practices and his focus on direct and indirect contact with many G.U.I.D.O.s, Ken was gaining a powerful side benefit of his efforts. Another G.U.I.D.O. was reaching out to him.

To Ken, counter-intuitive selling was starting to get very exciting.

The Successful Seven: Chapter 16
Action Steps for Mastering the Art of Counter-Intuitive Selling

1. Realize that a G.U.I.D.O. is the **highest-level individual** that we deal with inside our target prospect and customer organizations.

2. Understand the significance of the "D" element of G.U.I.D.O. **Effective delegation is key** to a G.U.I.D.O.'s success.

3. Look for ways to **indirectly establish your relationship** with a G.U.I.D.O. and with his executive assistant/gatekeeper.

4. Even before you establish contact and a relationship with a G.U.I.D.O., look for **opportunities for visibility** with him or her.

5. Use your relationships with H.E.R.B.s and H.A.N.K.s to **gain both direct and indirect access** to G.U.I.D.O.s.

6. **Validate a G.U.I.D.O.'s most pressing initiatives and problems** through multiple H.E.R.B. and H.A.N.K. relationships.

7. **Leverage your visibility and relationships** with G.U.I.D.O.s to gain access to additional G.U.I.D.O.s. **Let your actions and integrity speak for you.**

chapter seventeen

Once You Know Who's Who, It Is Time for Counter-Intuitive Action!

Understanding the characters outlined in the Decision-Maker Rater is the first step; taking action to change who you are dealing with is next.

Armed with an understanding of the acronyms and characters of the Decision-Maker Rater, Ken was thinking with a clarity and purpose that he never felt in the past. His mind was racing with thoughts as he finally understood why so many N.E.R.D.s had prevented him from landing a lot of the business that was sitting in his forecast.

Ken had been spending his I-Team appointments during the last few weeks reviewing his accounts, pinpointing N.E.R.D.s that were creating a "danger zone," and, most importantly, formulating plans to find H.E.R.B.s and H.A.N.K.s inside these customers and prospects.

In addition, it was refreshing for Ken and his sales manager to talk a common language about the contacts inside Ken's key targets and current customers. Now, instead of giving his sales manager a long explanation, Ken would just simply say things like, "I've realized that my main contact is a N.E.R.D., so I've already identified and met a key H.E.R.B." Life was suddenly much clearer and simpler, and this left more time to take action, which Ken really appreciated.

Putting All the Pieces in Place

Reviewing each and every account currently in his pipeline, Ken started to formulate plans to weed out N.E.R.D.s, establish relationships with H.E.R.B.s and H.A.N.K.s, and gain visibility and awareness with G.U.I.D.O.s.

These plans also applied to the new opportunities Ken was just beginning to work. He would make sure that he steered clear of forming any relationships with N.E.R.D.s. He would aim higher and look for H.E.R.B.s and H.A.N.K.s to guide his efforts and get him close—directly and indirectly—to G.U.I.D.O.s.

Inside the accounts where Ken currently had a relationship with a N.E.R.D., a H.A.N.K. and a H.E.R.B. created a nice decoy and a nice alternative path to a G.U.I.D.O. By finding and working with either a H.A.N.K. or a H.E.R.B., it would be less readily apparent to a N.E.R.D. that Ken was attempting to work around him or her, even though this was exactly his game plan. A direct route to a G.U.I.D.O. would definitely threaten a N.E.R.D., whereas the path through a H.A.N.K. or a H.E.R.B. could be explained to a N.E.R.D.—if necessary—in a number of ways.

The work Ken was starting to do with Zucor, a large pharmaceutical that was high on his target prospect list, was a perfect example of how—through H.A.N.K. and H.E.R.B.—Ken could create a situation in which N.E.R.D. was becoming less and less important. In addition, H.E.R.B. was beginning to lead Ken to several G.U.I.D.O.s (Zucor has several separate companies under its corporate umbrella and each one has its own G.U.I.D.O.) that were now ready to join some of the discussions and meetings.

Things were starting to fall into place at Zucor, and N.E.R.D. was not even feeling threatened. He just kept doing what N.E.R.D.s do best: focusing on unnecessary details for exorbitant amounts of time, finding reasons to delay the project, and trying to make decisions based on personal favors that Ken and Ken's competitor's salespeople would bring to the table. Ken was not comfortable with this way of doing business, so he was doing everything he could to leave the world of N.E.R.D.s behind him.

Ken was learning that H.A.N.K.s and H.E.R.B.s were both respected by G.U.I.D.O.s—often for very different reasons. A H.E.R.B. usually appeared to be a highly visible rising star within the organization. Often, a H.E.R.B. was someone on a fast track to additional responsibilities and promotions or someone new to the organization in a critical position. A G.U.I.D.O. viewed a H.E.R.B. as someone he could count on to deliver on critical projects and initiatives—initiatives that often started the company off in a new direction. A G.U.I.D.O. often described a H.E.R.B. as someone who was "helping us take the organization to the next level."

On the other hand, a H.A.N.K. was often someone that a G.U.I.D.O. looked to as an expert in a specific area, often referring to a H.A.N.K. as the "resident expert" on this or that. Many of the H.A.N.K.s Ken met appeared more soft spoken than the H.E.R.B.s. This did not make the H.A.N.K.s any less valuable to G.U.I.D.O. or to Ken; it was just a difference in personalities that Ken noticed.

Ken often found a H.A.N.K leading a progressive and forward-thinking HR department, running a procurement department that thought differently about vendor selection, or running a pet project for a G.U.I.D.O. When he would set meetings with a H.A.N.K., Ken would almost always walk away with a wealth of information that he had no idea at the time would end up being critical knowledge when it came to moving the relationship and the business forward.

There was another interesting trend that Ken began to uncover. A "real" H.E.R.B. and H.A.N.K. almost always respected each other, talked highly about each other, and looked for ways to jointly further the key efforts of the organization. This was something that was rarely true with a N.E.R.D., and not always because a N.E.R.D. was deliberately trying to sabotage key initiatives (although sometimes this was sadly the case). In most cases a N.E.R.D. was just not well enough connected or well enough "in the know" to understand how to impact these initiatives. A N.E.R.D. was often an outsider to what was really key to the organization's longer-term success.

Ken was also learning a lot about G.U.I.D.O.s—things he never realized in the past. The biggest lesson was what he had learned from Frank, his key mentor. The phrase "as high as appropriate, not always as high as possible" was etched in Ken's mind.

Even so, Ken created the following behavior trigger to keep this foremost in his mind. He placed one on his cell phone with a label maker, and one on his computer screen in his office. Whenever he was making calls to his target prospects and customers, this message was within view:

> **As high as appropriate**
> **Not always G.U.I.D.O.**
> **Create visibility and**
> **awareness with G.U.I.D.O.**

Ken was no longer automatically attempting to make immediate contact with a G.U.I.D.O. He was focused more on visibility with a G.U.I.D.O., along with indirect communication and contact (we'll cover more about this in Chapters 31 and 32).

Being the CEO of Your Own Destiny

Now that Ken was beginning to really understand the worlds of N.E.R.D.s, H.A.N.K.s, and H.E.R.B.s, he was beginning to look for new and different approaches in order to increase his success rate. Ken had been in the sales game long enough and he was growing tired of the old numbers game. He could sense he was beginning to leave that game by working smarter, not just harder. His conversations with target prospects and customers had changed dramatically, and Ken was feeling more relaxed and more in control of his own destiny.

Once again, Ken found himself thinking about his key mentor, Frank, and something Frank would remind him of whenever he sensed that Ken wasn't producing at the highest level possible.

"Remember Ken," Frank would say in a very stern voice, **"you are the CEO of your destiny and your success. Make the right choices and take the right action."**

The Successful Seven: Chapter 17
Action Steps for Mastering the Art of Counter-Intuitive Selling

1. Use the language of the Decision-Maker Rater (G.U.I.D.O., H.E.R.B., H.A.N.K., and N.E.R.D.) to **shorten and clarify** your account and prospect discussions with your sales manager.

2. Review all current customers to **identify the "danger zones"** created by N.E.R.D.s and to create strategy plans to identify H.E.R.B.s and H.A.N.K.s that can increase your odds of success.

3. Review all target prospects currently in progress to *quickly* identify N.E.R.D.s that could **potentially cause you to lose business** that you know is there to secure.

4. Use all of your upcoming I-Team appointments to conduct your account reviews, and do this **until all accounts are reviewed** and new strategy plans are completed.

5. **Do not engage** target prospects until you have properly planned to avoid N.E.R.D.s during your initial contacting efforts.

6. Realize the **commonalties as well as the differences** between H.E.R.B.s and H.A.N.K.s so you quickly and correctly identify each of them within your target prospects and accounts.

7. **Use behavior triggers to force necessary behavior change** as you enter this most critical phase of the journey into the world of counter-intuitive selling.

part three

Dialog That Sets You Apart—
Even from Your "Old" Self

Conversations That You Have Never Had Until Now

Talking differently with
your prospects and
customers

chapter eighteen

Letting Customers Know That They Are <u>Not</u> Ready

Sometimes, you need to send a "wake-up call" to your prospect or customer, telling them that—in your professional opinion— they are not ready to reap the rewards of doing business with you. Sometimes, that startling statement is the tipping point.

If Ken landed this deal with Zucor, it would be his second major win with one of the world's largest pharmaceutical companies. Thousands inside the organization needed his solution. Ken had just a few challenges to handle before he could successfully land the deal.

For one, he had a more expensive solution than anything Zucor had used in the past, and more expensive than what it was using now. In addition, Ken had a more customized and tailored solution and not all of the benefits were readily apparent on the surface. Ken needed to do something big, and quickly.

Fortunately, Ken had an opportunity, because he was back for a meeting with all of the H.E.R.B.s, H.A.N.K.s, and G.U.I.D.O.s that would use his solution (the typical committee-styled process that focuses on these decisions—you probably see this all the time). Only this time, the audience had grown. Joining the group today would be several more key business division heads (G.U.I.D.O.s) and the CIO of one of the largest divisions (a H.A.N.K and a G.U.I.D.O. all rolled into one). Ken's use of *PowerNotes* (a counter-intuitive selling tool that you will learn more about in Chapter 32) had paid off in creating indirect awareness with several more G.U.I.D.O.s, and today this indirect awareness turned into direct involvement with their attendance in the room.

The opportunity appeared to be in Ken's hands. He could win big or lose big today. Ken needed to create a startling event to take this where he needed it to go.

You see, in reality, Zucor's current solution was working well for the company, or at least it appeared to be working well. The lack of any obvious problems gave Zucor a no-risk solution that was easy to continue using, and like most companies, it was ready to stick with its current solution for this very reason.

It was time for Ken to shake things up a bit.

Using Counter-Intuitive Techniques to Shake Things Up

As everyone sat down after introductions and some catching up, the head of contract services (who at first appeared to be one of our champions, but who in reality Ken realized was a N.E.R.D.), laid out the agenda. No surprises, it was the usual stuff.

"First," N.E.R.D. began, "I'd like Ken and his team to review what they have proposed, and then I'd like all of us from the Zucor side to pose our questions and concerns. We'll open up the floor and spend the remainder of the time to sort through the items you have all sent to me prior to the meeting. I sent all of these along to Ken, so he and his team should be prepared to address everything." With that she looked at Ken, giving him the floor.

If Ken had started to address all of the concerns that the Zucor people around the table had listed in their "discussion points" lists, he would be doing what the typical sales professional would proceed to do—that is, the typical sales professional who had not yet entered the world of counter-intuitive selling. Most salespeople believe that by addressing the questions and issues they will win the deal. The reality is that this is a highly unlikely outcome.

As salespeople, we like to fool ourselves into thinking that these lists of questions indicate interest on the part of the customer, and that this interest means there is a deal at hand. By following the cus-

tomer's request and answering the issues and questions, we are allowing the customer to direct the situation when, in reality, **we need to
take control at this critical point in the sales process**, or risk losing the
deal forever.

The lists meant that N.E.R.D. was looking to create a situation in
which the Zucor team was, in their minds, reinforcing their former decision on the solution currently in use, thereby convincing the team *not*
to make a change. At the very least, N.E.R.D. would present enough issues to draw out the process so that a new decision could *never* get
made. How often (let's be honest now!) does this happen to you?

Ken began speaking.

"Thank you, Lois. I appreciate the time everyone took to put together the topics we want to cover today, so before we spend too
much time on all of this, I'd like to share a significant concern that
has developed in my mind. I am concerned about whether or not Zucor is ready to adopt the solution that we have proposed. From our
experience, we've learned that in order to adopt this type of solution—and truly reap the rewards, both financial and otherwise—the
client must be firmly committed to the solution and willing to work
with some out-of-the-box thinking. Based on the questions we reviewed, I felt I needed to share this critical red flag. We want to do the
right things here, and we'd rather walk away now than start down a
path without the right mindset among your team. This must be successful—for all of us."

Ken had just launched his number one missile and he was waiting
for the return fire. He knew it would come from one of the more senior G.U.I.D.O.s in the meeting, and it did.

Watching the Response to Learn All You Need to Know

The head of the largest division was the first to speak up (although the CIO looked ready to chime in as well). "What," she
started, "makes you draw this conclusion, and, more importantly,
what exactly do you mean by this?"

"Jeanette, I'll be candid," Ken responded without hesitation. "It's
the nature of the questions. These are the types of questions we tend

to get when an organization is not prepared to think differently about solving these issues. Now, we should talk more to delve into this deeper, but if this is the case, my recommendation is that you just stay with your current solution. And perhaps we can revisit this at some point later next year."

Jeanette fired back, "Why later next year? What do you think will change on our end?"

Ken recognized his approach was beginning to work and it had started them thinking *differently* because the CIO (a H.E.R.B) chimed in. "Ken, I want to understand which questions raised the red flag in your mind. Let's see where we need to go with this."

Ken was off to the races. He started to point out all of the questions that "raised the red flag" and emphasized his concerns. The tipping point was at hand and Ken was taking the opportunity to capitalize on it.

He quickly disregarded any and all questions regarding the "higher cost" of his solution by pointing out that this is where the Zucor team needed to start thinking outside the box. Ken emphasized again and again with them: "In order to see the total investment advantage here, let's remain focused on the overall impact to the organization: the streamlined process, the potential to redeploy your people that spend unnecessary time on this now, and the ability to impact other related areas, some that we have not even discussed to this point." The discussion was quickly approaching the point where everyone in the room was getting on the same page, so Ken needed to make sure that everyone on the Zucor team would stay there.

He needed to make his next move, so he launched his second missile.

Creating a Champion

It was critical for Ken to make sure N.E.R.D. was neutralized and not in a position to control how discussions progressed once this meeting ended. Looking right at N.E.R.D., he began, "In order for this to work the way we all want it to, and to make sure we continue along the path that we are now on, we need an ultimate owner of this within Zucor. It needs to be someone on the Zucor team who relays the decisions from your side, speaks for the committee, and interfaces with the final decision process team. Who should this be?"

Ken watched for what he knew was about to happen. N.E.R.D. naturally turned to the most senior individual in the room from the Zucor side. Until this point, Ken wasn't totally sure who this really was. As we've all learned (or should learn as quickly as we can), titles don't always tell us everything we need to know about the inner workings of an organization. But Ken was about to find out exactly what he needed to know to secure the deal.

N.E.R.D. looked straight at the head of the largest business unit and said, "Jeanette, this either needs to be you or someone appointed by you."

BINGO! Ken had confirmation that Jeanette was the senior G.U.I.D.O. in the room.

Until this point in the meeting, Ken was not sure if the CIO or the head of the largest business unit held the most power within the organization, but N.E.R.D. answered the question for him by responding as she did to the question. Now Ken was ready to nail things down and move forward with the deal.

Jeanette immediately responded, "Lois, based on these discussions today, that person should be me. Ken's right, this needs to be successful, and it needs the right attention. Let me take the lead."

If Jeanette had not stepped up and taken the lead, Ken would have asked her who she was appointing to be the lead person from the Zucor side, while gently encouraging her to be that individual. In the end, Ken would not leave the meeting until he had established his direct relationship with Jeanette, enabling him to call upon her at any time the deal even *hinted* at potentially stalling or heading south, and to make sure she remained engaged and in the mix. Ken's work with PowerNotes had done the job up until this point, so now it was time to leverage their effectiveness into a direct communication channel with Jeanette.

Ken's goal was simple: he quickly wanted to turn G.U.I.D.O. (Jeanette, in this case) into his biggest internal champion at Zucor. You see, the higher up in the organization your ultimate champion sits, the better!

There's more on this critical step in the next chapter; but first, take a moment to complete The Successful Seven for this chapter.

The Successful Seven: Chapter 18
Action Steps for Mastering the Art of Counter-Intuitive Selling

1. Utilize counter-intuitive **startling events** to change the course and direction of the sales process in order to remove a N.E.R.D. from a position of control.

2. Leverage your relationships with H.E.R.B.s and H.A.N.K.s **to gain visibility and awareness** with G.U.I.D.O.s—enough visibility to lure G.U.I.D.O.s into critical discussions.

3. Move the prospect away from the "easy out" decision to remain with their existing solution by posing the *"you're not ready for this"* startling statement.

4. Engage the G.U.I.D.O.s and H.E.R.B.s in the meeting to **begin to neutralize** a N.E.R.D.'s control of the sales process.

5. Move the control away from a N.E.R.D. by asking, "Who should lead this?" and then involving the N.E.R.D. in the **transfer of power process**.

6. **Gain commitment from the new leader** on the customer side before the meeting concludes.

7. Use the meeting as a vehicle to **strengthen and secure your direct relationship** with the new leader on the customer side.

chapter nineteen

Why Semantics Are Not Merely Semantics in the Counter-Intuitive World

---

As you continue to master the art of the unexpected, you will quickly learn a most important distinction: how you say things becomes *more important* than what you are saying.

Ken was learning quickly as he progressed into the world of counter-intuitive selling. He was becoming keenly aware of a very important fact: how you say something is just as important, perhaps even *more important*, than what you are actually saying.

Ken was also realizing that there are two sides to counter-intuitive selling. The first was obvious: **do the opposite of what the prospect or customer expects you to do**. But there was the less obvious side to counter-intuitive selling that Ken was realizing more every day: **you also must do the opposite of what *you* might naturally do**. This was an even more powerful side of counter-intuitive selling, as Ken was about to learn.

Learning Not to Sound Like a Salesperson

Frank had introduced Ken to counter-intuitive selling—piece by piece—and had the uncanny ability to know when Ken was ready for more, and when he wasn't. This approach over time (remember *time-spaced repetition* from Chapter 1?) allowed Ken to master what was important within counter-intuitive selling—step by step.

As he thought about Frank's lessons, Ken reached deep inside his briefcase and pulled out a piece of paper that he kept in the secret compartment. It was worn and tattered, but he still reached for it every so often.

On the tattered piece of old paper was the following:

> Counter-intuitive: do the opposite of what you might naturally do.
>
> Rather than pound from the outside, encourage them to reach from the inside.
>
> Rather than tell them, let them figure it out.
>
> Rather than trying to break down their resistance, allow them to break through it themselves.

Ken had written this down during one of his very first conversations with Frank about the art of counter-intuitive selling. Frank had been hesitant to share a lot at first. He wanted to be sure that Ken was ready.

To this day, Ken still remembers the conversation. "Ken," Frank had said, "you need to be prepared to change your long-standing behavior, and to see the prospect's behavior change as well. A lot of this will depend upon your ability to say things differently than you do today."

"**It's important that you do not sound like a salesperson**, because you are not a salesperson. You are on equal footing with the G.U.I.D.O.s on which you call. As a matter of fact, I would argue that you are actually holding the upper hand because you have something of value that they need. They just don't know it yet!"

Ken could sense that Frank was on a roll, so he just let Frank continue as he tried to take in everything that Frank was sharing.

"Ken, it's all about **sounding like you are at G.U.I.D.O.'s level**; that you belong. I can't tell you how turned off I get, or anyone in my office gets, when we pick up the phone and we can immediately tell that the individual on the other end of the phone is a typical salesperson, and a pretty mediocre one at that."

Ken's head was full of questions. "OK, I'm not sure I understand all of this. What do you mean by not sounding like a salesperson? And what do you mean by being on equal footing with a G.U.I.D.O.? How do I get there?"

Frank replied, "For one thing, you get there by continuing to interface with more and more G.U.I.D.O.s. The more you listen to them and interact with them, the more of their traits you will take on. Go where they go, read what they read, think about what they think about."

Ken was not sold on how to get there. "How do I get there? Come on, really, Frank. I can't talk to G.U.I.D.O.s all day, so what do you mean by 'go where they go, read what they read, think about what they think about'?"

As Frank started to reply, Ken sensed that he was about to get another "mentor moment" from Frank. In other words, Frank wasn't accepting something that he just heard from Ken.

"Wait just a minute, Ken. What do you mean that you can't talk to G.U.I.D.O.s all day? I guess if you think you can't, then you can't. You need to think differently. Think about what would happen to your business if you did talk to G.U.I.D.O.s all day! Who ultimately makes the decisions?"

"Most G.U.I.D.O.s lead a lot of community efforts, so get involved. But I must emphasize again: only do it if you believe in it, otherwise you are only kidding yourself. By the way, you won't be kidding the G.U.I.D.O.s. They'll see right through you. When you get involved, really get involved. Offer to head a committee, take on a tough task for a G.U.I.D.O. He'll appreciate your efforts and he'll begin to get to know you."

Ken began to see exactly what Frank was trying to teach him. He wanted more. "Frank, what about what a G.U.I.D.O. reads? Where do I start there?"

Frank continued. "A G.U.I.D.O. reads the *Wall Street Journal*, for one. He reads other business publications and gets information off the Web as well. Stay 'tuned in' to the business world and the financial world. This will give you a lot to talk about with G.U.I.D.O.s. As you talk with them more, they'll begin to see that you are 'tuned in' to their issues."

Becoming Comfortable in G.U.I.D.O.'s World

Although all of this was making a lot of sense to Ken, he decided to take Frank back to the beginning of the conversation.

"How does all of this have anything to do with not sounding like a salesperson? Honestly, Frank, I'm afraid I'm a little lost in all of this."

"Ah, this is the most critical point," Frank responded. "Don't feel lost. It's about to all make sense."

"Once you know how G.U.I.D.O.s think, what they do, where they spend their time, and how they talk about things, you'll be familiar with G.U.I.D.O.s. When you're familiar with G.U.I.D.O.s, you will be comfortable in their world; and when you are comfortable, you will begin to sound familiar and relaxed—just like a G.U.I.D.O."

"Ken, read all of the interviews with G.U.I.D.O.s that you can get your hands on. **Start talking the way G.U.I.D.O.s talk. Listen for the words they use, and take note of the topics they talk about and how they talk about these issues.**"

Although Ken did not realize it, Frank was about to share the most crucial piece of advice that he would share with Ken from this entire conversation.

"Ken, what do most salespeople do when they try to get a G.U.I.D.O. on the phone? You know what they do, right? 'This is so and so, from such and such company, and I'm trying to reach Mr. So and So.' What do you think most G.U.I.D.O. assistants think at this point?"

Ken tried to follow Frank's thinking. "G.U.I.D.O's assistant is probably thinking, 'It's another salesperson trying to reach G.U.I.D.O.' and he or she will probably shut it down right there."

"Exactly," Frank responded, obviously pleased with his student's response. "Instead of sounding like all of the other salespeople trying to get to a G.U.I.D.O., you need to do something different—something counter-intuitive. When you call for a G.U.I.D.O. and the assistant picks up the phone, try something like 'Is he in?' First of all, you sound familiar. You sound like you know G.U.I.D.O. Secondly, and here's the important part, you don't sound like every other salesperson who calls. This sounds easy—easier than it will be to actually put it into practice. It will take a lot of preparation and a lot of practice before you start calling G.U.I.D.O.s and taking this approach."

If this were true, then Ken knew what he would spending some of his upcoming I-Team appointment time working on for the next few weeks. He would not only read a lot of G.U.I.D.O. interviews, he would practice the "Is he in?" approach.

Ken thought he had a potential challenge, especially if this approach started to get him to G.U.I.D.O., so he had one final question for Frank.

"OK, Frank, this all sounds good, and I think I can master this approach. What happens when it works? What happens when I actually get a G.U.I.D.O. on the phone?"

Once again, Frank sounded quite pleased with the intensity with which Ken was tackling the counter-intuitive approach he was unveiling. "This is another key turning point in your counter-intuitive education. The key will be when a G.U.I.D.O. stops you by asking, 'Who is this?' This will be music to yours ears, and a sign that you are indeed on the right track!"

The Successful Seven: Chapter 19
Action Steps for Mastering the Art of Counter-Intuitive Selling

1. Realize that **how you say something** is even more important than what you say, and begin to think in counter-intuitive ways about your conversations.

2. Be prepared to **spend considerable time** changing your long-standing behaviors (habits) of what you say in sales conversations. Take advantage of your I-Team appointments to accomplish this.

3. Do things to **get on equal footing** with G.U.I.D.O.s. Go where G.U.I.D.Os. go, read what G.U.I.D.O.s read, think about the things that G.U.I.D.O.s think about.

4. Make a personal commitment to get **highly involved** in one significant community service organization or activity. Chose one that you believe in and make the commitment to get actively involved.

5. Use your I-Team appointments to **read as many G.U.I.D.O. interviews** as you can possibly get your hands on.

6. Begin internalizing the **"Is he in?"** response to G.U.I.D.O. assistants, so that when you begin calling for G.U.I.D.O.s you significantly improve your odds of getting G.U.I.D.O.s on the phone. *Remember that sounding familiar is the key!*

7. Prepare for the next chapter by realizing that it will take a lot of **time-spaced repetition** practice to break your long-standing habit of sounding like a salesperson.

chapter twenty

Why "Who Is This?" Is Now Music to Your Ears!

For most of our sales careers, we've had it all backwards. What we **by habit** tell our prospects *first* does not matter to them at all—until we let them know something much more powerful and significant.

In *MindsetMARKETING*, I teach select sales professionals how to completely change their initial phone conversations with decision makers (and gatekeepers!). Although the changes are relatively simple for me to explain and seem logical to the participants, adopting them is **the hardest new habit for most salespeople to form**.

Let me share an exercise we complete in every session of the training program, because I believe it will explain the challenge we all face in this area. We start the exercise by asking each participant to share the opening statement they use when they get the right decision maker on the phone.

After each participant shares his or her dialog, we quickly tally up the startling statistic that comes out of this exercise. Most (historically over 95 percent) sales professionals spend the first 20 seconds or more of this precious phone time stating the following four things:

1. Their name
2. Their company's name
3. The business
4. Their phone number

In reality, none of this means anything to the person on the other end of the phone. IT MEANS NOTHING! In interview *after* interview *after* interview with decision makers, they agree that this information is immaterial to them, and hearing it usually results in them "tuning out" the person on the other end of the phone, or simply hanging up. We usually have one or more senior decision makers in the session to validate this point, making sure that all of the participants hear this firsthand from the person they might be calling next. We focus a lot of energy on driving this point home to each and every participant.

In the next segment of the training program, we divide the participants into small groups and give them hours to revamp their opening dialog. We give them all the tools they need, including a customized version of the Counter-Intuitive Power Message Formula (*which you will learn about later in this chapter*) to steer them away from mentioning the four points listed above in their "new" opening dialog. We have them practice in pairs, practice in groups of three, and again in groups of four. After several hours of this, we have them deliver their "new" opening dialog to real decision makers.

Can you guess what happens?

I would love to report to you that most of the participants nail their "new" dialog after all of this practice, and that they flawlessly deliver their new message on target. The reality is that over 90 percent (I guess we're making some progress!) go back to mentioning at least two of the four points above within the first 15 seconds of their dialog.

Why is this?

Although what they are practicing makes perfect sense to them and is even backed up by the decision makers in the room, this new behavior is foreign to them. This counter-intuitive technique is **so foreign from anything they have ever practiced** in the past that it is almost impossible for them to move away from their current behavior and habits and adapt to the new thinking.

Creating a Counter-Intuitive Power Message

Think about it. If you have been in sales for even a relatively short time, perhaps just five or six years, you have talked to thousands of prospects and been trained in ineffective behaviors dozens of times. Mentioning who you are, what company you are with, and what you do is an ingrained, learned behavior. You do it without even thinking about it, just as you get in the car and head home from the office or another familiar place without thought about what you are about to do. You've practiced for years, you've perfected your delivery (perhaps subconsciously), and now you want to change?

The keys to change are the **desire, a plan, and continued repetition**, but you know all this from Chapter 1 (remember time-spaced repetition?). Let's start with the formula for your new Counter-Intuitive Power Message, and then we'll look at an example.

Counter-Intuitive Power Message Formula

Ten-Second Opening: When you connect with the right individual, allow that person the opportunity to clear his or her mind and focus on what you are about to say. Without this little opening to your *Counter-Intuitive Power Message,* your audience might miss a vital element of your message.

Your Credibility Statement (Your Right to Have the Person Listen): Share something—a fact or trend—that other decision makers of this individual's level and stature have shared with you and will find intriguing. Strike a cord of relevance in the mind of your audience.

The Thought-Provoking Question: Ask a question that transfers this fact or trend to your audience's unique situation and business. Bring it to a relevant and personal level.

Gain Commitment to Meet and Continue the Conversation: Pose a question that portrays mutual interest to meet. You need to find out more, the individual needs to hear more, and this small investment of time will be of value.

Understanding How the
Counter-Intuitive Power Message Works

As you look at this formula, what is missing? You guessed it! You don't mention any of the four items we discussed earlier. There is no mention of:

1. Your name
2. Your company's name
3. Your business
4. Your phone number

Why? The answer is simple, as we discussed before. All of these pieces of information are **completely irrelevant to the decision maker** on the other end, until that person decides differently. There is also a side benefit. The reason most decision makers will tune into this counter-intuitive approach is simple: when you master this approach, you will sound unlike the majority of the salespeople that the decision maker finds himself or herself engaged with on the phone—*if other salespeople even get the opportunity!*

Here's a proven sample of an effective Counter-Intuitive Power Message that has produced a significant amount of new business. Notice how it follows the formula:

> "Jack, thanks for taking my call.
>
> *(Opening)* Let me share with you why I am calling.
>
> *(The credibility statement)* I've been talking with other executives in organizations similar to yours, and they have been sharing with me the fact that they have spent a lot of money on technology—hardware and software—and they aren't sure if there is a real impact to the bottom line of their business.
>
> *(The thought-provoking question)* I imagine that you may be wrestling with the same questions and concerns, realizing that the key is the ability of people to put knowledge to work through this technology—is this an accurate assumption?

(The commitment to meet) I'd like to share with you how we are helping companies like yours get a return on these dollars you have already spent. I am not sure of the fit with your organization, but I believe it is worth a few minutes of our time to explore."

How will you know your counter-intuitive approach is beginning to work? You should look for one key indicator. This indicator is the moment when the decision maker on the other end of the phone (usually while you are in the middle of your thought-provoking question) interrupts you and says something like, "Who is this?"

Once this happens, you have **struck a chord of relevance** in the mind of your audience. Your counter-intuitive selling techniques are beginning to take hold, and you are about to enter a completely new world of *increasing the odds* of landing significant new business. You are now ready to practice a lot more counter-intuitive skills, as we'll learn in the next chapter. First, however, be sure to complete this chapter's action steps as you continue to refine your Counter-Intuitive Selling habits.

The Successful Seven: Chapter 20
Action Steps for Mastering the Art of Counter-Intuitive Selling

1. Realize that **breaking your current habit** of starting every initial phone conversation and phone message by stating your name and your company's name will be a hard habit to break.

2. Use the **Counter-Intuitive Power Message Formula** to create your personalized message.

3. **Do not deviate** from the proven formula.

4. Find yourself a "**sales buddy**" either within your sales team or from your network of sales professionals—someone who is as committed to excellence in sales as you are.

5. Work with your "sales buddy" to **critique and refine** your Counter-Intuitive Power Message.

6. Practice delivering your Counter-Intuitive Power Message to your "sales buddy" for 21 consecutive days **before** you make your first call to deliver it to a targeted decision maker.

7. Use the power of **behavioral triggers** and **time-spaced repetition** practice to make the Counter-Intuitive Power Message a habit.

chapter twenty-one

Sometimes They Want to Do Business with You, but They Just Don't Know How to Start

---

The counter-intuitive selling professional guides indecisive
prospects along the path toward a deal, and then
grows the opportunity over time.

In Ken's pursuit of mastering the art of the unexpected, he was quickly realizing that many potential customers need expert guidance in making decisions that will help solve their issues and problems. Once again, Ken found himself returning to one of his earlier conversations with Frank.

Frank was talking about *who* he did business with and *why*.

"When someone makes it easy to do business with them, the decision-making process is easier and faster," Frank said. "I get very frustrated when I think there is value in what someone presents— something that can really help our business—but it is not clear how to put things into motion. Many times in the past I've probably engaged with what turned out to be the second- or third-best solution, just because the salesperson who brought me the best solution didn't show me how to get started."

Ken asked Frank the question that was burning in his mind. "So, how does someone make it easy for you to do business with them? What do they do that most other salespeople fail to do?"

Frank thought for a minute, and then responded, "Good question and I think the best way to help you understand is by sharing an actual example that happened not too long ago."

"Ken, do you remember when I was spending all my time—at least what seemed to be all of my time—on the project to replace our system for our operations unit? Well, that was quite an involved undertaking. We began by reviewing our requirements and improving our processes, and then we started to take a look at potential systems that met our basic criteria."

"Frank, I remember that time all right." Ken said, recalling how extremely frustrating it had been for him, as well. "It was almost impossible during those six months or so for us to find time on your calendar. I was so glad when the project ended."

When Frank responded, Ken realized from the tone in his voice that another major "mentor moment" was just around the corner. "See, Ken, that's what's so amazing; the project is nowhere near complete. It just looks that way to you because I am no longer consumed by it."

Making It Easy to Do Business with You

Ken felt a bit lost as he tried to understand where Frank was going with this story, and how it fit in with his earlier words about easing the decision-making process.

"So what happened?" Ken asked. "Why are you not spending time on this project the way you were, especially if it is nowhere near complete?"

"First, let me tell you what changed and where we are today with the project," Frank continued. "We were talking to all of the top providers of solutions that fit our needs, and we had even narrowed it down to the top three or four. We were having all of the vendors in for half-day sessions, and I must tell you, each had impressive solutions. But every time we'd regroup as a committee after the meetings with each vendor, we always had the same discussion. In one way or another, we'd all be saying 'good solution' or 'nice fit' or something similar. However—and here's the key—when we would try to move to a discussion of how we would start doing business with that vendor, we'd just stall. Other than signing the contract, which every vendor was pushing us to do, we could not get comfortable with taking the next step in getting things rolling!"

"So what finally changed?" Ken asked. "How did you get to where you are today? The project is still in full swing and yet you are not consumed by it."

"Well, when I say we experienced the same thing with all of the vendors, I should say we experienced it with all but one," Frank continued. "This one salesperson was different; Victoria's her name. Before we realized it, **she started walking us through how we would engage together and get things rolling**. She asked us a lot of what I would call—if I was an attorney—leading questions. While she was doing so, she also shared insight into how this approach worked with many of her other clients. **In the end, she made us feel like she knew how to proceed every step of the way**, how to make sure we weren't the ones trying to figure it out, and—here's one of the most important pieces—**she gave us peace of mind** that she'd done this many times before with very solid results."

"So that was the end of it, the end of the story?" Ken asked, thinking this was the end of the mentor moment.

"Not quite. In our debriefing meeting, our team felt quite differently about the meeting we had just had with Victoria. My team could actually visualize what we needed to do next and what the outcome would be. It was obvious they had a lot of faith and trust in the sales rep that had just been there with us—meaning Victoria. The committee members were actually moving ahead in their minds, seeing our company using the solution."

"But here's the icing on the cake," Frank said. "As we were sitting in the meeting having this discussion, a message came over my Black-Berry. It was from Victoria. Here's what the e-mail read:

Frank,

Thank you again for the time with your team. The continued insight from your team is helping us to make sure we propose the right solution to your need. I imagine that you are discussing our meeting, or will be soon, as a team. If your team comes to consensus that our solution is viable, then I would suggest that we set a time to continue this discussion. I'd also like to make sure that if anyone who is part of this decision-making process was not available for the meeting today, we do not hold the next meeting without them. Their buy-in and thoughts are too important for us to continue without their involvement.

If there is one thing I've learned in working with clients like your company, it's that there is no perfect solution out there for you—not even ours. Therefore, the key comes in making sure we follow a process, as I outlined today, to make sure we match the solution to your needs and that our team, rather than yours, takes this burden on so you are free to focus on your core business.

I will call you in the morning to discuss next steps with you. Thanks again for your vote of confidence in our ability to deliver the results you expect from a potential partnership between our organizations.

Best regards,

Victoria

"As soon as I read Victoria's note, I was able to turn to the team and say, 'Victoria's already followed up, and here's what she recommends as our next steps, if everyone is comfortable taking a next step.' At that point the team was ready to continue discussions, and quite frankly all of a sudden it put Victoria and her solution a step ahead of any of the others we were talking to."

"Frank," Ken asked, "it sounds like a lot happened in those meetings—the meeting with Victoria and the one with the team—that you didn't share with me yet. What did she do? How did she get you to visualize using her solution?"

Frank thought for a minute, and then responded, "You know, it was more in the way that she asked us questions about how we would move forward and then continuing to ask more specific questions."

Using Questions to Lead the Customer Toward Your Solution

Asking leading questions is a powerful counter-intuitive selling tool. Leading questions encourage the prospect to begin visualizing the process of doing business with you. Tailor these leading questions for your selling situations. For example:

- If you were to take the next step—to see if what we proposed will actually deliver what you need—who will lead the effort from your team?
- Is there a functional area or team that will actually own this solution and be responsible for its everyday effectiveness and long-term impact?
- Does that team meet on a regular basis and, if so, when do they meet next?
- Can we schedule 20 minutes to be part of that meeting to hear their thoughts and concerns?
- How will you know, once we meet with this team, if they are satisfied that what we propose will fit your needs and be a workable solution?
- What areas of your organization will this touch that we have not included to this point, and when can we meet with them as well?
- Who from your team should we work with to set up regularly scheduled status meetings so that the right members of your team and our team work together to make sure this is the right solution and that the implementation is effective and delivers the required results?

Establishing a Plan for Success

In their mentoring conversation, Frank had gone on to explain to Ken why asking leading questions was an important tool for guiding a potential customer toward a deal.

"Ken, **Victoria was leading us**. You see, she was actually getting us to do what we ought to be doing anyway, but for some reason, we weren't necessarily inclined to do on our own. **She was making it easy for us to do business with her**."

Ken was once again completely lost for a second, and asked, "What did you mean by what you just said about 'getting us to do what we ought to be doing anyway'?"

Frank summed things up for Ken as best he could. "You see, Ken, the committee and I knew we needed to find the solution that would work for us, and we knew we needed to move forward because, until we actually did something, we weren't solving the problem that faced us."

"So that's it?" Ken asked.

"There's a little more. A G.U.I.D.O. wants to work with someone that has a plan—**a plan for success**. He wants to know that the person he's about to commit business to has done this before—implemented and achieved results. Victoria did this well, and she put my mind at ease enough for me to say to our committee, 'What do you think team? I'm thinking Victoria brings a pretty good solution that in the end will make a difference. Should we move forward?' And they couldn't come up with a good enough reason *not* to work with Victoria and her solution."

The Successful Seven: Chapter 21
Action Steps for Mastering the Art of Counter-Intuitive Selling

1. **Never assume** that just because a high-potential prospect agrees that you have a solution to fit their need that they also know **how to start doing business with you**.

2. Lay out a clearly defined "**process for engagement**" that you share with the prospect or customer early in your discussions.

3. Make it easy for your prospect or customer to engage with you, and place the **burden of easing that engagement on your team,** not their team.

4. Use **leading questions** to get the prospect or customer actually moving down the solution path with you. They will let you know if they are not ready.

5. Demonstrate through the process you share that you have delivered results and that you know how to take the burden off of the customer, allowing them to **focus on their core business**.

6. Make sure that **each and every person** that is either involved in the decision process or who will play a leading role in the everyday implementation of the solution is part of your discussions. **Do not proceed** until this happens.

7. Follow up your critical meeting with a counter-intuitive e-mail that outlines the next steps, and do so **the minute the meeting concludes**.

When Building a Relationship Is Best Done from a Distance

Thinking differently about how you reach decision makers

chapter twenty-two

Building Your Value Through a Virtual Relationship

Today's business climate makes it more challenging to reach
the people you need to reach. But today's technology and the
good old telephone—when put to work in counter-intuitive
ways—can give you the edge you need.

Ken had been on the trail of G.U.I.D.O. at Grey Scientific for
months. He felt like he knew Joan, G.U.I.D.O.'s executive assistant.
He had talked with her, however briefly, numerous times during these
months. Joan had indicated that G.U.I.D.O. would be in on this
morning and potentially available to take Ken's call, so he dialed
G.U.I.D.O.'s number and waited for Joan to answer.

"Joan Framingham," she said when she picked up the phone.

"Is he in?" Ken responded, highly practiced by now at the art of
sounding familiar, especially to Joan.

"Yes, he is," she answered back quickly, adding, "Is this Tom?"

"No, should I be Tom?" Ken was quick to keep things moving, re-
membering his goal was to get her to put the call through to
G.U.I.D.O.—his real name being Jerry in this case—before she
started to think too much about it. He continued his pursuit. "Can he
take my quick call? You mentioned this might be a good time for
him?"

"Is that you Ken? You sounded for a minute just like Tom Higgins
from the board, and Jerry said he needed to talk to Tom immediately
if he called—hopeful thinking on my part." Then she went back to fo-

cusing on Ken. "You know I saw the research paper you sent him sitting on his desk. Is that your work?"

At this point Ken realized that his **virtual efforts** to become familiar to Jerry were beginning to have their desired effect, and he started to feel good about this morning's events thus far.

"Not exactly my work Joan, but related to what I need to talk to Jerry about, so can you connect me?" With that, Ken waited to hear Jerry's voice as he picked up the transferred call. Instead, he got a most unexpected response from Joan.

"Actually, Ken, he is in his office, but you don't want to talk to him right now." Then she added, "Trust me."

Do Your Counter-Intuitive Detective Work

It was time for Ken to become the counter-intuitive detective. He knew from experience that this was the time to ask Joan to tell him more but not in so many words, and then to suggest he get back to Jerry at a time Joan suggests.

"Hmm, sounds serious, Joan. What's happening there at Grey Scientific? But before you tell me, it certainly sounds like your boss has more urgent issues to deal with right now, so please tell me when you suggest I try calling back."

"He just announced to everyone that we are collapsing several divisions into one," Joan said. "You know how these things go. Although everyone kind of knew this was coming, it's always hard when it first becomes official. He had to handle the displacement of some key individuals this morning, so he just told me he needs a few hours to piece things back together in his office. If I put you through, I don't think he'd be receptive to anything much right now."

Ken wanted to make sure that he and Joan stayed on track and did not get caught up in the emotion of the moment, so Ken quickly reminded Joan of the last part of his question. "Joan, I really appreciate your guidance here. As you know, I've always taken your advice. When do you recommend I call back?"

Ken could hear Joan flipping through Jerry's calendar on her desk, when she said, "You know, next week he's out for the board meeting and the finance meeting until Thursday. When he gets back in on Thursday he has a few things very early, and then he looks really good after nine. Why don't you call around 9:20 and I will make sure I get you connected with him then."

Ken was quite sure that Joan controlled Jerry's calendar, and this was confirmation of his suspicion. He now knew, as he did in most cases with other G.U.I.D.O.s, that Joan was the key to securing any time with Jerry.

Not wanting to jeopardize the opportunity to get this firm a commitment from Joan, Ken responded quickly. "Looking at my calendar, I have a meeting that morning. I will make sure I schedule a break and give you a call at that time—9:20. Thanks for the recommendation on when he and I can connect."

Then Joan said something most interesting. "Ken, thanks for understanding. I'm a little tired of people calling and demanding to talk to Jerry no matter what I try to tell them. You obviously get it."

Building a Virtual Relationship

So why was Joan so warm and receptive to Ken on this morning when he called to connect with Jerry? Did she just happen to open up to him about what was happening at Grey Scientific, or was there more to this than meets the eye?

In reality, this conversation between Joan and Ken was based on *months* of Ken's calls in which he simply asked Joan, "**Is he in?**"

When Joan would reply that Jerry was not available and then ask the question all executive assistants ask next, Ken would just stay on track and in control by asking, "Is there a better time for me to try to reach him? Is there somewhere on his calendar that we can pencil in a few minutes?"

Ken's counter-intuitive goal was simple, and he made sure he stuck to it: **offer as little information** as he could possibly get away with and **nail down a time** to call back when G.U.I.D.O. will be available. Ken also let Joan know that there is no need for him to leave a number, because G.U.I.D.O. will have just as hard a time reaching Ken, and G.U.I.D.O.'s time is too valuable to be spent chasing down Ken.

Are you confused yet? Does all of this make sense?

You Are Busy—With Little Time to Talk

Let's go back to one of Ken's "mentor moments" with Frank. It was the time when Frank said to Ken, "A G.U.I.D.O. wants to deal with someone who is just as busy as he is."

When one G.U.I.D.O. calls another, it is usually a battle of trying to get two very busy people with hectic schedules together—a great challenge for the two executive assistants. When you relay that you are just as busy, **your importance grows** in both the mind of the G.U.I.D.O. and the mind of his or her executive assistant.

Whenever Joan would say, "Let me have your name and number, so he can call you back," Ken would always respond this way: "My schedule is extremely hectic, and I would hate to see G.U.I.D.O. waste his time trying to track me down. When does his schedule look open, so that I can have a brief conversation with him?"

At this point, during one of the first "Is he in?" conversations, Joan would ask, "Will he know who you are?"

Ken had learned the most effective response to this, so he would answer, "I'm not sure if he'll recall. My name's crossed his desk, at least, and his colleagues may have mentioned me to him." Once again, Ken was becoming a **master of familiarity**, as we call it in the counter-intuitive world.

Ken was also mastering the art of another key counter-intuitive trait: **always being busy, no matter what**. Always reminding Joan that G.U.I.D.O. would not be able to reach him if he tried to call was enough for Joan to appreciate that Ken was very aware of not wanting to waste G.U.I.D.O.'s time. Joan is the ultimate protector of G.U.I.D.O.'s time; it is her number one job as his executive assistant.

Become the Resource G.U.I.D.O Didn't Know He Had

There was a third element here, in addition to the key elements of building familiarity and always controlling the fact that you will get back to G.U.I.D.O and *not* have G.U.I.D.O call you. This is the element of becoming a source of expert and timely information to help G.U.I.D.O.'s thinking and his business, even before you meet with or talk to G.U.I.D.O.

Do you remember Joan mentioning to Ken, "I saw the research paper you sent G.U.I.D.O. sitting on his desk"?

When Ken made the decision that Grey Scientific was a key target prospect and that he would launch the "Is he in?" campaign to speak with G.U.I.D.O., Ken also became a resource to G.U.I.D.O.—one he didn't even know he had at his disposal. Once Ken learned a little bit about Grey Scientific and the issues that G.U.I.D.O. was dealing with in the business, Ken started sending him valuable information.

Although Ken didn't maintain a regular schedule of sending information to G.U.I.D.O.'s office, his contacts were **regular and consistent**. He never went more than three weeks without sending something. More importantly, the information Ken sent was unique and had high potential value to G.U.I.D.O.

Sometimes, Ken would send an obscure article from the *Wall Street Journal*, something G.U.I.D.O. might not read fully as he scanned the paper each day. Sometimes the information was a white paper or research paper from a well-respected firm. Other times, Ken forwarded a published interview with a prominent CEO who was dealing with similar issues, or something about a new technology that could assist G.U.I.D.O. in his efforts.

Ken also varied the delivery method of the resources and the designated recipient. One time, for example, he might e-mail the material to G.U.I.D.O. Another time, he might overnight a printed version to Joan, with separate notes for Joan and G.U.I.D.O. This way, Joan felt included. She would remove Ken's note to her, leave the note to G.U.I.D.O. on the material, and place it on the top of the stack on G.U.I.D.O.'s desk.

Ken has three objectives to achieve with his "resource service" to G.U.I.D.O:

1. **Provide value**, so G.U.I.D.O. begins to view Ken as valuable, even though he really does not yet know him.
2. Begin to leave a **trail of "impressions"** with both G.U.I.D.O and his executive assistant (we'll talk more about the importance of impressions in Chapter 31).
3. Begin to **build the "air of familiarity"** with both G.U.I.D.O. and his assistant, so that when they finally connect, Ken is not a stranger to them.

Integrating these objectives into Ken's daily habits as a counter-intuitive selling professional also helps Ken achieve the number one counter-intuitive selling objective: **he no longer *looks*, *feels*, or *acts* like a typical salesperson.**

The Successful Seven: Chapter 22
Action Steps for Mastering the Art of Counter-Intuitive Selling

1. Be prepared for a **campaign of "Is he in?" conversations** with G.U.I.D.O.'s executive assistant before you ever connect with G.U.I.D.O.

2. Use the conversations with G.U.I.D.O.'s executive assistant to **build familiarity and awareness** with G.U.I.D.O.

3. **Never leave your number** with G.U.I.D.O.'s assistant—share that you are extremely busy and that you do not want G.U.I.D.O. to waste his time attempting to reach you.

4. Always gain from G.U.I.D.O.'s assistant a **time that looks good** on his or her calendar for you to call back and connect with G.U.I.D.O.

5. Become a "**resource service**" to G.U.I.D.O. and make sure that what you send to him or her is **unique and valuable** as it relates to the issues inside the business.

6. **Vary the delivery** of the information you send G.U.I.D.O.s. Use e-mail, overnight deliveries, and Priority Mail.

7. While you should send a large majority of the information directly to G.U.I.D.O., be sure to also **send some of the information to his or her assistant**, and include a personalized note for each of them.

chapter twenty-three

Why Single Sales Letters No Longer Work—and Should <u>Not</u> Work

---

Sales letters are one of the most overused tools ever invented, and they simply *do not work.* Most sales letters never get opened before they're tossed as junk mail.

Ken had learned a lot from Frank about how salespeople could get Frank's attention on the phone, or the attention of his executive assistant. Ken now also realized that any attempt to reach a G.U.I.D.O. would involve a campaign, and not a single contact.

He was now wondering how this applied to letters he might write to a G.U.I.D.O. Was there something important that he needed to learn from Frank about sales letters as well?

Ken had actually stopped writing sales letters. He found letters to be totally unproductive and a waste of time and effort. He even thought about it from the G.U.I.D.O.'s perspective. "If I were a G.U.I.D.O., would I read what I send out?" Ken knew the answer to that question was no.

Recently, however, Ken had wondered, are there sales letters that Frank reads that actually get his attention? Because he was having his monthly lunch with Frank in a few hours, he was about to make sure that this was the first topic they covered today.

How the Typical Sales Letter Fails

As they sat down at the restaurant, and after some of the usual catch up, Ken started the series of questions that he hoped would end his curiosity. "Frank, what do you do with letters that you get from salespeople? I imagine you get quite a few. Do you actually read any of them, and do you ever call a salesperson based on a letter that you get?"

"Never," Frank said. "Typical sales letters are just that—sales letters. As a matter of fact, my assistant, Tim, tosses away most sales letters without even opening them. **You can tell by the envelope, by the metered postage—just by the look and feel—that it's a typical sales letter**, so into the garbage it goes. We get hundreds every week or so."

"Great," *Ken* replied. "That answers my question. I gave up on sales letters a while ago, and you've just confirmed that they don't work."

"Actually, not so fast," Frank was obviously thinking back on something, reaching back in his mind to share something profound with Ken. Ken was ready for another mentor moment.

"Do you remember Victoria from the company that we recently awarded our business to for the administration system?" Frank asked.

"I do. Victoria—the sales pro with the plan. The sales pro with the process to engage you down the path of doing business with her. How's that going by the way?"

"Right, the sales pro with the process to engage us in doing business with her. It's going great," Frank said, getting back to Victoria. "As a matter of fact, it's going better than I expected—like clockwork. **It's all about expectations**, you know. Victoria set expectations up front. She said there'd be bumps, but that we'd handle them as a joint team, and that's *exactly* what we're doing." Frank paused, and then asked, "Did I ever tell you how we first found out about Victoria and her solution?"

"No," Ken said. "I don't think you did. I just assumed she was a vendor that you called in when you decided you needed the right solution to solve the issues at hand."

"Interesting that you say that." Frank grew more animated as he spoke. "Actually, we didn't even *know* about Victoria or her solution. We didn't even know her company *existed.*"

Building Relationships Through Counter-Intuitive Campaigns

This comment surprised Ken; had Frank's company awarded a business contract to a company of which they had no previous knowledge? "If you didn't even know about her, how did she get into the mix?"

"It actually started a few months before we awarded the business to Victoria and her team," Frank said as Ken listened intently.

"One morning, I received a one-page letter in a FedEx letter envelope. Actually, it wasn't really a letter. Well, I guess it was a letter. Anyway, it was one page that talked about key issues I was wrestling with at the time. The letter was only signed with a name, and the letter let me know that I'd receive a few more like it over the next month."

Ken became more curious. "So what did the letter say about Victoria? I mean, it must have at least mentioned her company, what she does, and all that stuff."

"**Absolutely not**—not a thing about any of that," Frank responded. "It just made some points about issues that I was actually thinking about on an almost daily basis, and then the comment that I would be receiving a few more of these over the next month or so. Then there was the most interesting point about this letter; it actually said that Victoria was not going to call me."

Having no idea where all of this was heading, Ken needed to start asking Frank some questions. "I don't get it. Victoria sent you a letter that told you nothing about her company, and it actually said that Victoria was not going to call you. Why would she do this? It makes no sense."

Looking across the table and smiling at Ken, Frank continued. "Actually, it makes a lot of sense to me now. As I mentioned, Victoria's first letter told me that I would be receiving a few more over the next month or so, and I did—almost like clockwork about every ten days or so."

"What were the next letters like?" Ken asked, excited to learn where this was all heading. "Were the others just like the first one?"

"Yes and no. Each letter got a little more specific about issues that we were facing and to each one Victoria attached something else to read—once it was a white paper, another time a case study, and I remember another one had an article from *Harvard Business Review* attached to it. I remember that one clearly, because I even had Tim circulate the article to my team."

"So why did you even read these letters, or whatever they were?" Ken wanted to understand what prompted Frank to read these above all of his other mail, especially above any other "sales letters."

"I'll have to show you one or two of them the next time we're at my office," Frank said. "I'd have to say it was everything about these letters that made me want to read them—the look, the feel, the tone. These letters were all business and focused on business issues. Then there was the presentation. Victoria sent these on high-quality paper. Her letters weren't even formatted like a normal letter. You'd have to see one to understand."

"What else about these letters attracted your attention? Why did you open them?" Ken prompted Frank.

"Ah, glad you asked." Frank looked pleased that Ken reminded him to make this point. "The letters never arrived the same way. One time it was by FedEx, one time it was Priority Mail, another Express Mail. One time I think she must have actually dropped it off in the mailroom, because it looked like the internal mail I get from other department heads. Victoria's letters never arrived looking like a sales letter or junk mail."

Ken realized that lunchtime was about to end; both he and Frank had places to be, so he started to wrap up the conversation. "Frank, it sounds like Victoria's letters really had an impact. They obviously did, because you gave her a big piece of business as a result of her efforts.

I think I'll try something like this, but I think I'll just try it with one letter."

Frank's expression changed from his normally calm demeanor to one that was stern and somewhat disappointed. "You're missing one of the key points of this entire story, Ken, and I am a little disappointed in you. Let me ask you something: If you and I talked once on the phone, would you consider that we have a relationship?"

Ken was really wondering what could possibly be coming next. "Why, of course not, Frank."

"Exactly!" Frank fired back at Ken. "So why on earth do you think that one letter would do the trick to start a relationship with someone? Ken, **it's all about the relationship**. Victoria was forming a virtual relationship with me. It's all about the relationship, Ken—the relationship!"

The Successful Seven: Chapter 23
Action Steps for Mastering the Art of Counter-Intuitive Selling

1. Commit to the realization that **typical sales letters are dead**— especially single sales letters.

2. Design all future sales "letters" as a **campaign of multiple letters** over a period of time.

3. Make sure your letters **look unique** (a suggested format is shared in Chapter 25) and are devoid of typical sales information including your title, your company's name and address, and your business phone number.

4. **Vary the delivery method** of each letter in your campaign. Use Priority Mail, Express Mail, FedEx, UPS overnight, and internal departmental mail delivery, if possible.

5. Use timely research papers, white papers, case studies, and articles as support material to your letters.

6. State clearly in your first "letter" that you will **not be calling G.U.I.D.O.** until a later point in time.

7. **Space the mailing** of your "letters" out to allow for about ten days between the mailing of each letter in your campaign.

chapter twenty-four

Recurring Impressions Connect the Dots in the Mind of Our Target Decision Maker

---

Time-spaced repetition—a key to your success in acquiring counter-intuitive selling behaviors—is also a key in building a virtual relationship with your target accounts

---

As Ken learned from Frank, most sales letters lead to a dead end. The letters are tossed without being read and nothing follows them, unless it is a call from a salesperson inquiring, "Did you get my letter?"

Are you smiling yet? How many of your letters in the past were probably never even opened by the person to whom you sent them?

Now, imagine that you have sent a series of letters that look like no other letters and, unlike typical sales letters, hardly even mention you and your product or service. On top of that, imagine that your letters state, "We're not going to call you—at least not right now."

This is a counter-intuitive approach to selling; and it produces a letter that, more often than not, gets read.

Effective Ideas Are Sometimes Counter-Intuitive to Our Native Thought Process

Let's start with some cold, hard statistics from a sales professional who has been using these letters over the years, in industries ranging from software to professional services to telecom, and then the seminar/training business.

Listen to the results from her most recent "mini-campaign." In fact, this is the voicemail she left for me late one evening as she was wrapping up her week:

"Bill, just checking in at the end of a long week to let you know that I launched my second mini-campaign (she means that her campaign was targeted to a very small group of decision makers) and the impressions are working. I'm batting .350 in my attempts at getting in front of these folks; pretty good, considering that all other attempts have netted me nothing. The toughest one actually called me—well, her assistant did. I'll keep you posted; I know the percentage of success will rise as I take the next step. Talk to you soon."

Now, here's the challenge: three times in her career this highly effective sales professional has been asked to share her secret and her process with the rest of her sales team (or the entire sales organization, for that matter). Each time she's received that request, she has prepared her presentation on creating a counter-intuitive letter campaign, demonstrated how she executes the program, and explained what kind of results her approach produces. And each time, the same thing happens; in the end, her ideas are somehow dismissed. This same outcome has happened with three different, fairly well-known organizations where she has been a high-performing member of the sales team.

So what is her reaction, and what does she do? She smiles (she's prepared for the reaction by now), stops trying to convince the audience, and continues to reap the rewards of her counter-intuitive selling habits!

Why are the ideas and processes of counter-intuitive selling dismissed so many times? The reason is this is counter-intuitive selling at its best and, as such, it is so far removed from what we think of when we think of selling that:

1. We cannot grasp the concept; it does not fit in within our past experiences.
2. We cannot change our own bad habits and bad thinking to make it work for us.

Why Most Sales Professionals Overlook the Value of Counter-Intuitive Letter Campaigns

Ironically, there was only one time in my entire selling career that another organization grasped the uniqueness and the effectiveness of the counter-intuitive letter campaign. In that case, I was working inside an organization that had on staff two highly credentialed PhDs in organizational development and psychology with extensive backgrounds in human behavior.

I explained the campaign process and design with them, and even before I began to share results and statistics, one of them stopped me and said, "This is beautiful; this is the best sales tool I have ever seen, and it is obvious why this works effectively." Of course, he followed this with a lot of "psychology terminology" as I call it—stuff that was way over my head as a simple salesperson—but it was valid and it made a lot of sense, even to me.

One of those on-staff PhDs also explained to me that even the most seasoned sales professionals become programmed to the point that we find it hard—actually impossible—to think in counter-intuitive ways. It goes back to what we covered in Chapter 2 when we revealed how hard it is for us to make permanent changes in our learned behaviors. Even though we try and are sometimes successful—for short periods—at thinking counter-intuitively, we always slip back to the old habits. As a result, we also slip back to achieving the same old results—*inferior* results.

Connecting the Dots Through
Recurring Impressions

Although those with a PhD in psychology easily grasp the potential for counter-intuitive thinking, to get sales professionals to **think differently** about their sales letters and live contacts **is the key challenge**. Success with this approach has to do with subtle, recurring impressions and "connecting the dots" in the prospect's mind.

When we get a letter in front of the right decision maker (more on this in the next chapter) that is unlike any sales letter that person has seen before—it says nothing about us or what we are "selling"— we have our *first hook*. When we combine this hook with the fact that we let them know that we are *not going to contact* them, the power begins to build.

As the one PhD said to me, "We are playing tricks on their mind in a way that they can't quite figure out, and they are so intrigued that they begin to come along for the journey." In reality, these prospects are sensing and reading an approach that is counter-intuitive to everything they've ever experienced from sales professionals, so they find it refreshing and compelling enough to invest a few minutes. This is the **one and only goal** of our first contact with them: *to get them to respond in a simple way.*

Behind this initial letter are three more that follow—all delivered in different ways and all designed to "build a trail of impressions," as the one PhD described it. (We'll spend more time on the importance of impressions in Chapter 31.) The last letter has a most unique kicker added to it that we'll describe in full detail in the next chapter.

Delivery and Presentation Are
Just as Critical as Content

Here's one other key point about this highly powerful counter-intuitive selling weapon: delivery and presentation are just as crucial and critical as the actual content.

Not only have I learned this the hard way again and again (old habits begin to creep back into my behavior which I have to resist!), but the PhDs verified this as well; so pay close attention as we walk through the process, step by step, in the next few chapters. In fact, time and time again, I get calls from teams that I've worked with that go something like this: "Bill, we're midway through a campaign with your letters and the results are dismal—and I mean dismal. Far below what we've experienced in the past. We need some help to figure this out."

When they walk me through the details of how they are implementing the campaign, the problem is always the same. Without realizing it, they've changed something, usually something that appears subtle or unimportant to them. The reality, however, is that the little change or changes take them out of counter-intuitive thinking and back to the mainstream habits of salespeople, and therefore the campaign fails miserably. We'll talk more in future chapters about the critical warning signs that will alert you to when you start to slide back into old habits, so we make sure you stay on track in your counter-intuitive selling habits.

For now, however, consider the historical track record and the timeline of responses and interactions from the use of this campaign with targeted and highly challenging prospects (meaning these prospects never responded to any of our other efforts to contact them). You'll see how a certain percentage of the prospects with which you initiate the campaign "peel off" and actually reach out to you *before* you reach out to them. This is the 35 percent to which the salesperson you read about earlier in this chapter was referring to in her voice-mail message to me (when she said she was batting .350). When I consulted one of the PhDs about this, his response was, "This is typical human behavioral response to something unfamiliar, which is the essential beauty of this approach. The prospect wants more, and they want more now."

The results of these campaigns demonstrate the power of the counter-intuitive approach to sales letters and the importance of the multiple impressions, something we will explore in more detail in

Chapter 31. As with any counter-intuitive selling tool, these letter campaigns are meant to improve your odds. Nothing, including these letters, will guarantee your success. However, if you average a 50 percent success rate with these counter-intuitive campaigns, you are far ahead of the game as compared to your results before you entered the world of counter-intuitive selling.

Remember, the key for success here will be to stick with the proven design and process without letting your old learned habits and behaviors derail your efforts to be truly counter-intuitive in your new actions. But don't worry, we'll spend some time later in the book on ways to make sure you stay on track and reap the rewards of your new thinking.

Now that you understand some of the reasons why this approach is so effective, we're ready to get into the details of each of the letters and the process of the overall campaign. In the next chapter, we'll get to work on the actual letters in your "campaign of counter-intuitive impressions." But before we do, let's take time to complete The Successful Seven for this chapter.

The Successful Seven: Chapter 24
Action Steps for Mastering the Art of Counter-Intuitive Selling

1. Realize that there are very good reasons why **your sales letters of the past have not produced results** for you: all sales letters look and feel like sales letters, and G.U.I.D.O.s know that as well as you do!

2. Realize that counter-intuitive selling letter campaigns are **unlike anything else** in the world of professional selling, and therefore, these could be met with a high level of skepticism by other sales professionals.

3. It will take a lot of reminding with **behavior triggers** and practice to perfect your counter-intuitive selling campaigns.

4. The **one and only goal** we have when we launch our counter-intuitive letter campaigns is to get the prospect to respond in a simple way.

5. Remember that **presentation and delivery** of the letters in the counter-intuitive letter campaign are just as important as the actual letters.

6. As you learn and master the specifics of the counter-intuitive letter campaigns in the next chapter, make a commitment **not** to **vary from the proven formula**.

7. Use several of your weekly **I-Team appointments** to begin crafting your first letter for your counter-intuitive selling letter campaigns.

chapter twenty-five

Letters for a Lifetime Relationship

The impressions that you create through a time-spaced counter-intuitive sales campaign will result in some of your most important, longest-lasting customer relationships.

Ken was anxious to get a look at the letters that Frank had talked about over lunch, so when he was in the area the following week, he had set a time to drop by and take a look.

Frank mentioned that he would be in a meeting and probably would not see Ken while he was there, but he also made sure that he left the letters with Tim and also had a conference room reserved for Ken to examine the material.

As Ken retrieved the envelope from Tim and headed to the conference room, he noticed a small note attached to the envelope with a paper clip. The note read:

Ken—

Take a look. These are truly not what I expected or what I had ever received from a salesperson before. The first one arrived FedEx, then I think the next one was Express Mail, and then Priority Mail; I could have the order mixed up. The last one appeared to be delivered through interoffice mail.

Anyway, glad you're taking a look. I hope you learn something!

Regards,

Frank

Launching the Counter-Intuitive Selling Campaign

As Ken opened the envelope, he discovered that Frank had numbered each letter in the order in which it arrived. As Ken started to take a close look at the letters, he could see what Frank meant when he commented, "The letters from Victoria don't look like sales lettters."

The format was very different. There was no "to" or "from" address. Ken also noticed that the letters weren't originally dated, but that Frank had jotted down the dates on each one. "That's Frank," Ken thought. "Always the facts."

The letters were printed on high-quality paper, and there was another difference that Ken suddenly realized—no letterhead. The print was larger than normal and more elegant than most letters. As Ken held one of the letters, he thought to himself, "This just feels like it's quality."

Ken placed the letters out across the conference room table, and then picked up the first one. He looked at the letter closely and started to read it. (See the first letter on following page).

When he was finished reading it, he thought to himself, "Frank was right, there is no mention of Victoria's company and what it does. This letter is completely focused on issues that are probably of significant importance to G.U.I.D.O.—meaning Frank in this case."

As Frank pointed out, the letter also let him know that Victoria would not be calling him anytime soon. Then Ken noticed the "P.S." which talked about the article included with the letter. It was an article from *HRDirections* magazine and it featured a prominent head of human resources.

Although Ken wanted to study the first letter more, his curiosity had him wanting to look at the remaining three letters, so he went on to the second one. (See the second letter on page 162).

This letter appeared to get a little more specific about Victoria's company, only it did so through the use of a case study. Once again, Ken immediately noticed that this letter did not sound anything like any sales letter he had ever written in the past. Questions, quotes, and a case study are what made up this letter. This letter, like the first one,

"...whether you debate the semantics or even decry the concept itself, the bottom line is that human capital management will have a huge impact on, well, the bottom line..."
—Brian Grant, Editor-In-Chief
HRDirections, May 2007

Dear Frank,

With today's unstable business environment and the increased scrutiny by board members and shareholders alike, how do we ensure that our organizations are prepared to compete and excel in the critical years just ahead? How do we ensure that each individual is given the opportunity to unlock the potential business payoff that each brings to the table?

Human capital management (HCM), talent development, succession planning, competency mapping—*these are all terms being thrown around today as the current and next wave of corporate initiatives.* **But the terms by themselves mean little in return to your bottom line.**

We've strategically partnered with key organizations that are household names throughout the world with one goal in mind: **to increase the talent within the organization and create additional shareholder value and confidence, while enhancing the overall financial results.**

Over the next few weeks, we will share with you some of the compelling research on the subjects of human capital, talent development, and succession planning throughout an organization. We will also share the specific results we've helped blue chip organizations achieve.

You will not hear from us until you've had the opportunity to receive all of this information and share it with key members of your executive team, so don't expect to receive a call from us for a month or so. I trust that this valuable information will help you make the best critical decisions for the future of your organization.

Best regards,

Victoria

Victoria Benetti
Victoriab@kpinc.com

P.S. The attached article reprinted from a current issue of *HRDirections* details the initiatives underway at American InfoSystems, and the results achieved. If you'd like additional copies for your team, please call me at 1-800-123-4567.

"The most important corporate resource over the next 20 years will be talent. Not capital, not technology and not global distribution of markets."

—McBride & Company

Human Capital Report

Dear Frank,

Is your organization prepared for the future with the right talent to take your business to the next level of performance? Do you actually know what talent lies within your organization? Are there critical skill gaps that need to be filled? Do you have a road map for talent that ensures you can meet your business objectives?

These questions and more are what prompted the executive leadership team at Karney McDowell to partner with KnowledgePotential Inc. to create a comprehensive human capital initiative to transform the organization for the future.

Why KnowledgePotential Inc. for this blue chip company? In the words of Susan Walrus, executive director at Karney McDowell, *"KnowledgePotential's solution was, and is, unparalleled in leadership development circles."*

The enclosed case study, a joint project of Karney McDowell and KnowledgePotential Inc., provides an in-depth view of current research into the key subjects of human capital management, succession, talent development, and performance measurement. It also shares insight into the process Karney McDowell undertook, including the benchmarking of some of the most successful global organizations.

I hope you find its ideas useful.

Best regards,

Victoria

Victoria Benetti
Victoriab@kpinc.com

P.S. Our experience in working with focus groups across the United States in dealing with the challenges of human capital development may prove useful to you and your executive team. We welcome the opportunity to share the findings with you. I can be reached at 1-800-123-4567.

ended with a postscript—a reason that Frank *might* want to call Victoria—just an option for Frank.

From the dates that Frank had jotted on each letter, Ken noticed that the second letter arrived ten days after the first letter. He then picked up the third letter and read the date that Frank had written on it. Once again, the letter had arrived ten days after the previous one.

The third letter made Ken immediately think back to something that Frank had shared with him. Ken could still hear Frank's voice in his head. "Make it easy for me to do business with you, and you've almost made the decision for me!" This third letter focused on simplifying things by working with Victoria's team.

"Very interesting," Ken thought to himself. "This is exactly what Frank said was paramount in his decision-making process, and what resonated with his team."

The third letter talked about specific success stories, and was accompanied by a case study. The letter's postscript extended an invitation for Frank to attend an executive briefing that featured a G.U.I.D.O. from one of Victoria's client companies. (See the third letter on page 164).

Then Ken noticed something about all of the letters. Each letter started with a quote across the top, where a "normal" letter would carry the letterhead. It really caught Ken's eye and he just realized that this is where his eyes naturally went as he started to read each of the letters.

Establishing a Time for the First Call

As Ken picked up the fourth and final letter, he was curious to see how it was different from the preceding letters. (See the fourth letter on page 165).

"People of the caliber we're looking for are
pleased with the system—it gives them the opportunity to
outperform our expectations and meet their own.
We've enjoyed a record-breaking year in our largest division."

—Albert Costello, Sr. VP Human Resources

American InfoSystems

Dear Frank,

Facing changing customer tastes and demanding profit goals, American InfoSystems set out to overhaul its personnel policies, with human resources leading the way. Partnering with KnowledgePotential Inc. and incorporating the Talent Management Solution (mentioned above) into an overall strategy, American InfoSystems is realizing record results in its business units.

A key to success in an initiative of this caliber is aligning core values and strategic vision with the talent of the people inside the organization. Once the current talent levels are established, development plans can be created—all tying to the business objectives.

Sound complicated? It doesn't need to be.

Partnering with KnowledgePotential's team of leading, seasoned human capital development specialists can simplify your initiative and put it into the reach of each and every employee around the globe. We've worked with the best over the years, including AT&P, Zucor, Karney McDowell, and of course, American InfoSystems.

The enclosed case study provides in-depth analysis of the initiatives and achievements within American InfoSystems. It is essential reading for members of your team needing more detail into the underlying complexity of talent solutions that drive fiscal performance.

Best regards,

Victoria

Victoria Benetti
Victoriab@kpinc.com

P.S. We are embarking on a series of executive briefings, featuring Albert Costello of American InfoSystems. He will be sharing, up-front and personally, the initiatives inside American InfoSystems that led to these results. For more details, please call me at 1-800-123-4567.

*"We will continue to expand these initiatives
[referring to the LEAD program] and create others
like them regardless of business conditions, because
leadership and talent development are
too critical to our future success."*

Michael J. Cromley, Chairman & CEO, Karney McDowell
Letter to shareholders/annual report

Dear Frank,

Perhaps you have reviewed the information we have been sharing over the past few weeks, and then said to yourself, *"This is nice stuff, but it is not a priority right now..."*

Too critical to our future success?

Karney McDowell's Chairman and CEO was serious when he mentioned in the company's annual report and at its shareholders' meeting that these initiatives are too critical to their future to be on the back burner. And the results at both Karney McDowell and American InfoSystems speak for themselves: **American InfoSystems achieved record results in its largest division as a result of these initiatives.**

Our goal is very simple: we will work with you to analyze your major business challenges, design programs to solve these challenges, and work side by side with your people to produce measurable results.

The results we have shared with you over the past few weeks are real, and we have more success stories to share with you. More importantly, we are ready to work with you to build your success story—*a success story with significant return on investment.*

The enclosed KnowledgePotential Inc. fact sheet provides an overview of our strengths and our history. I've also enclosed the page from the Karney McDowell annual report where its CEO talks about the results we have helped the company achieve. I look forward to learning more about your goals and objectives when we have the opportunity to meet.

Best regards,

Victoria

Victoria Benetti
Victoriab@kpinc.com

P.S. I will call on Tuesday, August 13 at 7:40 am. If you will not be available, please let Tim know a good time for us to meet and discuss what I have shared with you. I will work with him to set an appointment on your calendar.

The fourth and final letter followed the same format as the other three. The look and feel was the same. The contents of the letter, however, seemed a lot more powerful than the first three letters.

"This letter really proves that Victoria's team does what Victoria says they can do," Ken thought to himself as he read the letter. "How much more powerful can you get than the story of the results that two different G.U.I.D.O.s gained from utilizing Victoria's solution? And it's all contained on one short page!"

Ken finally looked at the date that Frank had written on the fourth letter. Once again, letter four was dated ten days after letter three. Frank had received each letter exactly ten days apart from the previous one. The letter also mentioned that there was a fact sheet about Victoria's company attached with the letter.

The postscript on the final letter was a little different. This one told Frank that Victoria was going to be calling—on a specific date at a specific time. "I wonder what the significance of that is," Ken thought to himself, and then he immediately realized the significance. "How clever, or should I say 'how counter-intuitive!' When Victoria calls Frank on that date at that time, she can now say to Tim, 'Frank is expecting my call.'"

Ken looked at his watch. Although only half an hour had gone by since he stepped into the conference room with the letters, Ken felt like he had just received the education of a lifetime. As always, Frank's mentoring had exceeded Ken's expectations. Although Frank had not been with Ken for this half-hour, it was definitely one of the best mentor moments that Frank had ever orchestrated for Ken.

With a big smile crossing his face, Ken headed back to Frank's office. Although he realized Frank was locked away in meetings for the afternoon, he needed to return the letters. Ken was ready to immediately start putting counter-intuitive letter campaigns to work in his selling efforts.

The Successful Seven: Chapter 25
Action Steps for Mastering the Art of Counter-Intuitive Selling

1. Always start your letters with a **headline quote** from a well-respected source. The headline can hook a G.U.I.D.O.'s interest, so he or she will read more of your letter.

2. Use high-quality parchment paper and an elegant font. Remember that **presentation is as critical as the content**.

3. **Do not include the addresses** of G.U.I.D.O.'s company or your own company in your letters.

4. Address G.U.I.D.O. by **his or her first name**. Remember that equal footing is key!

5. Use short paragraphs and easy-to-read sentences. Talk only about G.U.I.D.O. issues in your letters.

6. Include a **postscript at the end of each letter**. The postscript in the final letter lets G.U.I.D.O. know when you will call his or her office.

7. Through your letters, prove to G.U.I.D.O. that you understand his or her issues and that you have **experience in solving** these issues. Do this through case studies and testimonials.

chapter twenty-six

Preparing for Surprising Results as the Tables Turn

You are now at a point in your journey into the world of
counter-intuitive selling where you can see how
the art of the unexpected begins to pay off.
Paying attention to the details is key.

After taking a close look at the counter-intuitive selling campaign
that Frank had received from Victoria, Ken's curiosity level was at an
all-time high. Ken was getting ready to write his counter-intuitive letters and decide on the small group of high-potential G.U.I.D.O.s that
he would target with his first campaign. Now, he wanted to know what
Victoria said when she called Frank, and how Frank had responded.

He waited until he knew that Frank would be in his car on the way
home, and then dialed Frank's mobile number. They often talked at
this time; it was good for both of them to spend this time winding
down from the day and sharing experiences.

"What did you think of the letters?" Frank started when he picked
up the phone on the other end. "By the way, my apologies that I could
not break away from my meeting. I hope Tim took good care of you."

"Frank, I knew you were booked all afternoon," Ken responded.
"So no need to apologize. And yes, Tim took good care of me, as he
always does. I spent about half an hour—time flew by quickly—looking at the letters and taking notes. You were right; these are really
unique. I haven't seen—and more importantly, I've never written—
any letters like these; but I will tell you, I plan to now!"

Then Ken added, "And don't worry, Frank, I won't try to shorten things by trying to do this with one letter, or even two or three. As you reminded me, it's all about the relationship, and a relationship is not going to be built with one letter."

"Just realize, Ken," Frank replied, "It's a lot more than the letters. At least I think it is. Victoria does her homework on the results her customers realize from her solutions, and she really builds her letters around those results—and I think it's key. So I don't think letters without the hard evidence that Victoria shares will work as effectively. She let me know, in a very short letter each time, that she could deliver results—and that she's delivered them for others."

Frank started to add to his thought, but Ken cut him off. "I know what's coming, Frank. Victoria was showing how she was making it easy for you and your team to do business with her."

"I see you're learning this quickly! Glad to see it's made an impression on you." Ken could hear the smile and satisfaction in his voice.

Making Phone Contact with G.U.I.D.O.

"So what's on your mind this evening, Ken? What do you want to talk about now that you've seen the letters and looked them over?"

Ken posed all of his questions at once. "Did Victoria actually call you? And if she did, what happened? Did you get on the phone with her? If not, did you call her back?"

"All great questions, Ken," Frank responded. "It's good to see how far you are thinking this all through. You're anticipating all the situations that can occur when you place your calls after your final letter in the campaign."

"Actually, Victoria did call when her final letter indicated she would call, and I was out of town."

"So did you call her back when you were back in town?" Ken interjected.

"No I didn't. As a matter of fact, Victoria has never asked me to call her back. She's always left the burden of the next step on her shoulders, and in doing so she's kept control of our contact. As I think more about it, this is a very smart move on Victoria's part. With how busy I am, I would never keep any commitments to call her back. It's not that what she has for me isn't important, it's just that I'm so busy all the time."

Frank was beginning to give Ken a complete picture of how things unfolded with Victoria. This all made sense to Ken, and he made mental notes as Frank shared how things had progressed with Victoria. He wanted to know what happened next.

"So did you end up talking with Victoria, and if you did, what did she say about her letters when the two of you connected?"

"We did connect," Frank said. "She just asked Tim when I would be back in town, and the two of them found ten minutes on my calendar that worked for both of us. She was absolutely great about working with Tim. He even commented to me about this. Several weeks later we connected."

"What did she say about her letters when you spoke with her on the phone?" Ken asked.

"As I think about it now, she said absolutely nothing about her letters." Frank then added, "I'm just realizing this right now; **she didn't say a word about the letters**."

"Then what did she say?" Ken was intrigued about Frank's realization.

"She was brief and to the point. She focused on the issue at hand and the impact she could have for us in this area," Frank replied. He continued, "As a matter of fact, it had slipped my mind that I was scheduled to talk with her, and Tim was out for the afternoon, so my direct line was forwarded to my cell line. I was walking out of my previous meeting when the phone rang. Victoria immediately talked about the issue and how she could impact our results, as she said she had done for her other clients. I finally said, 'Who is this?' She then laughed, explained who she was, and continued. I was listening, and what she was saying made sense."

At this point in the conversation, Ken had a mentor moment. He realized that *if* he could get a G.U.I.D.O. to interrupt him and ask,

"Who is this?" when he called following the final letter in the counter-intuitive campaign, he would be right where he needed to be.

The Continuing Importance of Behavioral Triggers

Ken now had a new goal. He decided to create a behavior trigger that he would post on his copy of the last letter in each campaign he launched. When he had the last letter in hand as he called G.U.I.D.O. at the time stated in the final letter, the following trigger would stare Ken in the face:

---

issue

impact

G.U.I.D.O.: "Who is this?"

Ken also knew that he should make sure he was fully prepared for his conversation with G.U.I.D.O. Things were about to change in a big way in Ken's world of selling, and he was feeling a little apprehensive—these were major changes and big steps in his career.

As Frank and Ken each approached their driveways, it was time to wrap up their conversation.

"I've really enjoyed this time, Frank. Thanks again," Ken shared as he was getting ready to head into the house to greet the family and enjoy a relaxing dinner.

"I have as well. It's exciting to discover new ways to build your business, isn't it? But something's bothering you, Ken," Frank said in his often fatherly tone, "What is it?"

"I don't know, Frank." Ken knew from experience that he couldn't fool Frank at a moment like this. "OK, I do know. This is a lot of good stuff, but it is very different. I'm not sure I can do this. I mean, I'm not sure that I can do it as well as I'll need to, in order to get to the right people."

Frank always knew how to get his student to step up and perform even better than Ken thought he could, so Frank took control and said, "Ken, do us both a favor, go relax with the family, get some sleep, and when you get in the car in the morning—if you are headed in early as usual tomorrow—call me. You know I'm out the door at sunrise, so let's connect then. We'll sort this out then. Have a great night, my friend."

With that, Ken grabbed his briefcase and headed to the house. He knew that his conversation with Frank in the morning would clarify things for him.

The Successful Seven: Chapter 26
Action Steps for Mastering the Art of Counter-Intuitive Selling

1. Make sure your counter-intuitive campaign emphasizes that it will be **easy for G.U.I.D.O. to do business with you** and your team.

2. Highlight **case studies and quotes** from clients that have benefited significantly from your solutions within your letters.

3. Be sure to call G.U.I.D.O. at the **exact time** you indicate in your final letter.

4. If G.U.I.D.O. is not available when you call, **work with his or her assistant** to secure ten minutes on the calendar when you can connect with G.U.I.D.O.

5. Never request that G.U.I.D.O. return your call. Keep the **burden of contact** and follow-up on your shoulders.

6. When you do connect with G.U.I.D.O. do not mention your letters. **Focus on the issue at hand** and how you can add value and impact for G.U.I.D.O. and his or her organization.

7. Remember the end goal in your first call: getting G.U.I.D.O. to interrupt you and ask, **"Who is this?"**

part four

Control Is Key—Perception Is the Art

Essential Elements of the Counter-Intuitive Mindset

Acting differently and
thinking differently:
The powerful counter-
intuitive combination

chapter twenty-seven

"As a Man Thinketh"

In the world of counter-intuitive selling, our mindset is as important as our actions. Model your mindset to mirror that of G.U.I.D.O. and you will greatly increase the odds of success.

As Ken headed out to the car while the sun was rising the next morning, he wondered what Frank wanted to talk with him about on the ride to the office. Knowing Frank, there was obviously something on his mind; Frank does not set time to talk without a purpose. Everything Frank does, he does with purpose. This has always impressed Ken about Frank.

As he closed his car door and headed down the driveway, Ken picked up his cell phone and dialed Frank's number.

Being Ready for Your Mission

"Good morning," Frank started this morning's conversation. "Did you get a good night's sleep?"

"Yes, I did, Frank. I took your advice and just enjoyed the evening with the family. There was a lot to think about and absorb yesterday, so it was good advice. Thanks."

"Ken, please do me a favor," Frank said. "Do you remember that little tiny book that I gave you? The one you said you'd keep with you in your briefcase at all times?"

"It's always in there," Ken responded, "It's there, along with a few tattered pieces of paper of my notes from our more important meetings."

"Good," said Frank. "Glad to see you are a man of your word. Do me a favor and pull it out. I hope you've pulled it out a time or two since I gave it to you. It's been a number of years, hasn't it?"

"Yes, it has," Ken said, pondering how long ago it was. "And yes, I pull it out every once in a while when I need to pause and gather my thoughts."

Ken pulled out the tiny book, which was no more than three inches by three inches in size. Although it was quite worn and scratched, Ken could still make out the four short words that graced the cover: *As a Man Thinketh.*

Frank continued, "Do you remember what I wrote inside the cover for you, Ken?"

Inside the cover Ken found the following:

> *To Ken,*
> *May you think that you can,*
> *and come to know that you will,*
> *succeed in whatever you desire.*
> *Frank*

"Are you there?" Frank asked after what Ken realized was a minute or two of silence.

"I'm here. I'm just thinking about when you gave this to me, and what was happening at the time in my career."

"Oh, I remember it well," Frank chimed in. "You were about to take on that assignment that you weren't quite sure you could handle—something about the experience of the team you were going to lead being so much more than your own. But look at what happened. That led to you landing the position you have now, with a much larger firm and a much better solution to offer to your customers. You did everything you needed to because you got the thought in your mind that you could!"

"So what are you trying to tell me now, Frank? As long as I think I can create these new letters, and as long as I think that I can talk to a G.U.I.D.O. when I get him or her on the phone, that I will be able to do all of this effectively?"

"Not exactly."

Ken began to feel that another mentor moment was just around the corner.

"I don't want to oversimplify any of this, Ken, but now that I've seen it in action, part of it is pretty simple. However, that doesn't mean it will always be easy; there is a difference. This will take a lot of practice on your end. Part of it definitely is believing that you can do this, and having the internal drive and commitment to go make it happen. So, it's imperative that you believe you can succeed with all of this, but there's more."

Frank went into his teaching mode as he continued, "The feeling I got from Victoria—and it started with her letters and went right through to the most recent meetings we've had with her—is this: she was **on a mission to talk to me about something that was important to my business**, and she was not going to stop until we had the discussion about it. It was her **mental mindset** that impressed me."

Ken asked, "Does this go back to what you've taught me about how you say something is just as important as what you are saying, and the discussion we've had on that subject?"

"Absolutely, and it even goes beyond that," Frank said. "It really has to do with putting yourself in this mental mindset: 'I have something very important to talk to G.U.I.D.O. about and I am on a mission to make contact. I will not relent until I get the meeting with him to discuss helping his business achieve even greater results.'"

Laugh Together and You Both Relax

"The other piece of advice I think will help you, Ken, is this," Frank added. "Keep it light, make the person on the other end of the phone laugh if you can—whether it's G.U.I.D.O. or his or her assistant or whomever—and I think you'll find that this relaxes both of you and improves your results."

"Make G.U.I.D.O. laugh," Ken repeated, half questioning the thought and half thinking it through. Then he asked, "So, did Victoria make you laugh when she first called you?"

Frank paused a moment, and then replied, "You know, come to think of it, I don't remember if I actually laughed but I found myself smiling. She certainly laughed, which put me at ease and changed the tone of our conversation. It happened when I stopped her and asked, 'Who is this?' She paused, laughed and said, 'My apologies for not saying who I was sooner.' Then she quickly said her name and went right back to sharing the point she was making about helping my company. I think we both did actually laugh about it, come to think of it. She was good!"

"Yes," said Ken, "and I am determined to be just as good at this. I've already started on my letters and I am setting aside my I-Team time for next week to practice—over and over—my calls to G.U.I.D.O. once he or she gets my final letter. I am going to make sure I am confident, ready, and prepared to do what it takes to reach him or reach her."

Your Mental Habits Are Just as Important as Your Physical Habits

Frank's tone indicated that he was pleased with Ken's response. "Now you're thinking in the right way, Ken. See, it is not only **your physical habits**—the things you do—that will improve your results; **your mental habits**—the things you think—will improve your performance as well. You need a determined mindset in order to be extremely successful at this, so here's what you need to commit to mastering in your mind and in your actions:

I have the skill and mindset to get a G.U.I.D.O.—one who does not yet know me—on the phone. Within two minutes, he will be convinced that it is critical that he continue the conversation with me and *schedule time to meet with me.*

"Remember, Ken, what you have to share is critical to G.U.I.D.O. I mean, I think about where we'd be if Victoria had never made contact. We certainly would not have the great solution we have today and we wouldn't be working with Victoria's great team."

Frank added one more thought before ending the conversation, and it turned out to be an important one. "Ken, remember something about G.U.I.D.O. He is a very positive thinker himself. He thinks about getting things done, and then he goes and gets them done—usually through his team. He's gotten to where he is today exactly because he thinks this way, and he wants to surround himself with people who think the same way. I guarantee you that once you get through to him and make contact, he'll be just as glad about it as you. The two of you will be on the same page, thinking the same way, and he'll appreciate your efforts and persistence."

Frank followed that statement with the most profound words of the entire conversation. "Ken, what you have to offer a G.U.I.D.O. is very important to him. As a matter of fact, if you don't get to him, you are doing him a disservice and you are not helping him get the most out of his business. You need to get to him, and get to him effectively. Remember, if you don't, your competitor will, at some point. Now, is that what you want to have happen?"

"Think about it, and call me when we have our next appointment. Tim has it on the calendar, if I remember. I'm off to Europe for a few weeks. When I get back, I want to hear about your progress. See you then."

With that, Ken opened his car door, grabbed his briefcase, and headed into his office. He was excited about all of the counter-intuitive tools he was gaining and he was anxious to get started putting the campaigns to work. He was also realizing that he had a lot of work ahead of him in order to master the art of the unexpected. He remembered that the key would be in his time-spaced repetition. He needed to get practicing, but only after he took care of the customers and prospects on his calendar for today—and the action steps for this chapter.

The Successful Seven: Chapter 27
Action Steps for Mastering the Art of Counter-Intuitive Selling

1. Remember that your mental habits—what you think—**are just as critical to your success** as your physical habits—what you do.

2. Commit to **maintaining the mindset** that will create your success. Think that you will succeed, know that you will succeed, and you will succeed.

3. **Commit to the mission**: you are on a mission to talk to G.U.I.D.O. about something that is important to his or her business, and you are not going to stop until you make contact.

4. When talking with a G.U.I.D.O. and his or her assistant, work to keep the conversation light. If you can laugh and **make G.U.I.D.O or his or her assistant laugh** with you, the entire tone of the conversation will change and any tension will be removed.

5. Commit your upcoming I-Team time to **creating and practicing** your initial conversations with G.U.I.D.O. Refer back to Chapter 26 to review what this conversation should sound like.

6. **Commit to the mindset:** I have the skill and mindset to get a G.U.I.D.O.—one who does not yet know me—on the phone, and within two minutes he or she will be convinced that it is critical that we continue the conversation and **schedule time to meet.**

7. Remember that what you have to offer a G.U.I.D.O. is very important to him or her. As a matter of fact, if you don't get to a G.U.I.D.O., you are **doing him or her a disservice** and you are not helping the G.U.I.D.O. **get the most out of his or her business.** You need to get to G.U.I.D.O.—if you don't, your competitor will.

chapter twenty-eight

The Age-Old Debate

How Much Research Is Really Necessary?

The amount of research you must do before contacting a
G.U.I.D.O. flies in the face of conventional sales wisdom.
This is one area in which the art of the unexpected will
lighten your workload!

While teaching select top selling professionals in the companion
sales training program for counter-intuitive selling known as Mindset-
MARKETING, I've had the opportunity to gather a lot of solid information about the amount of research an effective sales professional
needs to conduct before making contact with a G.U.I.D.O.

As it turns out, the results of our findings point to a classic case of
perception versus reality.

Counter-Intuitive Account Research: Perception vs. Reality

When we poll sales professionals in the preparation stage and ask
them how much research they need to do prior to making contact
with the target organization and the target G.U.I.D.O., the respondents overwhelmingly agree that the research is "critical" and should
be "extensive."

The respondents share the perception that they must gather detailed research and information on the target prospect. They also voice an urgent need to obtain and review the following about the organization they are about to contact:

- Size
- Number of employees
- Location of headquarters
- Locations of additional operations
- Executive leadership team members
- Board makeup and profiles of members
- Acquisitions over the past three years
- Annual sales
- Top initiatives
- Global expansion
- Annual reports for the last three years
- Press releases from the last 12 months

When the same sales professionals are interviewed after contact has been made with the target organization and the G.U.I.D.O., and initial meetings have been conducted, they express a very different perspective on the need for initial research. These same sales professionals, when carefully questioned about the impact and value of all of this "up front" time invested in research give a resounding answer: the research and information gathering added "little to no value" to their meetings, conversations, outcomes, and next steps with the prospect.

Why the significant gap between reality and perception when it comes to the topic of account research? Some interesting answers surface, so let's take a look at the key findings.

The first has a lot to do with the ritual that has been created during the past few decades surrounding "account research." Several well-known sales training programs have focused on account planning and development. All of these programs are solid and worthwhile programs, even though they may overemphasize the need to conduct extensive research prior to making contact with a G.U.I.D.O. and others inside the target prospect organization.

The counter-intuitive selling recommendation is that you keep a close eye on how much time you spend on account research; that time might very well turn out to be better spent in other areas, where it can yield a larger return for your investment.

Many sales professionals potentially waste time diving too deeply into account research because, as mentioned by our PhD friends from Chapter 24, *it's been **ingrained into our minds and habits** that all of this research is vitally important, so we find it hard to think otherwise.*

"Many sales professionals gain a false sense of security or pre- paredness from all of this research," one of the PhDs explained. "It is also a lot less threatening for the sales professional to spend time re- searching the account than it is to spend that same time actually con- tacting the key people they need to reach. Call it a fear factor—they won't face any rejection while they collect data—but they sure will face it when they get on the phone to talk to decision makers."

Knowing all of this, what should the counter-intuitive selling pro- fessional do when it comes to account research? Our advice is to keep it simple, and keep it brief.

Our recommendation is that before you head out to meet with a G.U.I.D.O., take a look at the latest annual report (if it is a public company) paying close attention to G.U.I.D.O.'s latest letter to the shareholders, and scan the organization's Web site for ten minutes before your appointment, looking for the latest quotes from G.U.I.D.O. This will arm you with any urgent information you need to know going into the meeting. Learn the least you need to know to get to G.U.I.D.O. and then "get on with getting to G.U.I.D.O."

Preparing for the Unexpected

For the counter-intuitive selling professional, it is far more critical to spend time looking for what we refer to as "unexpected events" and "impending events" that can change the urgency under which a

G.U.I.D.O. must tackle his or her priorities, or perhaps even change the G.U.I.D.O. in charge.

Unexpected and impending events include:

- Mergers and acquisitions
- Changes in senior leadership
- Regulatory changes
- Bankruptcies
- Lawsuits
- Hostile takeovers
- Earnings announcements

As a counter-intuitive selling professional, there is no more valuable or productive way that you can spend your time than by spending it reaching a G.U.I.D.O. and getting time on his or her calendar.

Learning the Most Effective Ways to Reach a G.U.I.D.O.

The most important information the counter-intuitive sales professional needs involves identifying and reaching G.U.I.D.O. Some of this information is readily available. Almost every organization's Web site includes a list of senior management, and some even include links to e-mail and more. At the least, the Web site should help you find out who's who among the G.U.I.D.O.s inside your target organization.

So how do we find out the rest of the information we need to know to be most effective at reaching G.U.I.D.O?

First of all, let's decide what we would like to know. It would be very helpful to know the following:

- The **name** by which the people who work with G.U.I.D.O. refer to him or her. In other words, if his name is Thomas, do people refer to him as Thomas, Tom, Tommy, or another nickname? Remember, a key is sounding familiar, and knowing a G.U.I.D.O.'s name is a big part of being familiar.

- The name of the **G.U.I.D.O.'s assistant**, so you can greet him or her when they answer G.U.I.D.O.'s phone.
- **G.U.I.D.O.'s direct number**, in order to avoid the screening that takes place at the switchboard and/or by the company operator.
- **G.U.I.D.O.'s e-mail address**. Although these are usually easy to figure out based on the company's e-mail address protocol, it is always nice to verify, just in case G.U.I.D.O. has a personal e-mail address at which he gets the e-mail he really wants versus a public e-mail address for all nonessential contacts.

How does the counter-intuitive selling professional gather this information—information that is, at times, highly guarded by gatekeepers whose job it is to keep this information out of the hands of just anyone who calls requesting it? Let's explore a technique that will give you access to this information.

The Counter-Intuitive FedEx Technique

This tool is known as the "Counter-Intuitive FedEx Technique" and it has been used effectively by counter-intuitive selling professionals for years. Here's how it goes.

Call the main number at the location where the G.U.I.D.O. has his or her primary office. Depending on whom you get on the other end of the phone and the time of day, you may want to experiment with the most effective time to call. We've heard from a number of highly effective counter-intuitive selling professionals that calling early in the morning or after business hours yields the best results. However, this counter-intuitive tool has proven to be effective at any time of day.

When you reach the person on the other end of the line, launch into the following:

"I am hoping you can help me. I have an overnight package for G.U.I.D.O., and as you can imagine, I want to make sure it reaches him in the morning. I'm sure you do as well. I've got the label in front of me, so can I just verify that I have all of the correct and needed information."

"I have the address as 123 Main Street, Metropolis, NY 10011. Is this what I need? [*Continue once they validate the information.*] The form also asks for his direct number. What is that? [*Write it down as the person shares it with you.*] Great, thanks. Oh, and it also asks for his assistant's name, in case G.U.I.D.O. is not in. What is that name? [*Write it down as the person shares it with you.*] Also I need the assistant's direct number, in case the package arrives there before the operator is manning the phones. [*Write it down as the person shares it with you.*] Great, I appreciate the help. One more thing: what does everybody call G.U.I.D.O? What name do his friends call him? [*Write it down as the person shares it with you.*]."

Once you've secured all of this invaluable information, you are ready and armed with what you need to effectively connect with G.U.I.D.O.

The Successful Seven: Chapter 28
Action Steps for Mastering the Art of Counter-Intuitive Selling

1. As a counter-intuitive selling professional, become keenly aware of **perception vs. reality** of how much research you really need to conduct before you attempt to reach a G.U.I.D.O.

2. Rather than prematurely spending valuable time gathering detailed research on a G.U.I.D.O. and his or her organization, focus on spotting "**unexpected events**" and "**impending events**" that can spell opportunity for the counter-intuitive selling professional.

3. Use **annual reports** and the news sections of the organization's Web site to uncover the latest quotes from G.U.I.D.O.

4. Make sure you gather the personal information you need about G.U.I.D.O. before you make your first attempt at contact. Pay close attention to learning the **preferred name** by which people call G.U.I.D.O.

5. Learn the name of G.U.I.D.O.'s assistant and be prepared to **greet him or her by that name** when the assistant answers G.U.I.D.O.'s direct line.

6. When all else fails, employ the "**Counter-Intuitive FedEx Technique**" to gather the needed information about G.U.I.D.O.

7. *Always* address G.U.I.D.O. by **his or her preferred *first* name**; *no last names are allowed in the world of counter-intuitive selling.*

chapter twenty-nine

Offering Up Too Much Spells Danger

Information sharing is a critical element of the art of the unexpected. The counter-intuitive selling professional always keeps control of the sharing of information while meeting with a G.U.I.D.O. and members of his or her team.

Far too many selling professionals offer up more information than is ever needed in their selling situations, sharing detail upon detail with a G.U.I.D.O. and others. Let's face it, salespeople love to hear themselves talk. This trait has killed many a sales career and many a selling opportunity.

Here are a few key principles that can help you, as a counter-intuitive selling professional, to limit information sharing to only that data that is extremely relevant to the discussion at hand:

- **Less is more** when it comes to sharing information with a G.U.I.D.O. and others, especially during your first conversation and your first face-to-face meeting.
- The use of the **counter-intuitive call agenda** assists in keeping the first meeting with a G.U.I.D.O. on track, by making sure that you play the role of *detective* or *doctor* (more on the role of "doctor" later in this chapter).
- All of the information that a G.U.I.D.O. shares with you during the first face-to-face meeting should be gathered with one thought in mind: creating the perception in the G.U.I.D.O.'s mind that you are an expert who will make recommendations *only* after you fully understand his or her situation and priorities.

The Counter-Intuitive Call Agenda

How many times during your professional selling career have you walked into a critical first meeting with a target high-potential prospect, only to hear the prospect say, in one way or another, "OK, tell me all about what you have to offer"? From that point forward, the prospect is in control, and no matter how you attempt to wrestle control back, the situation usually deteriorates from there.

The most effective way to avoid this situation and remain in control of the outcome of the meeting is to utilize the *counter-intuitive call agenda*, in which you would say something like this:

"Thank you for the opportunity to meet today. In order to make the best use of our time, I would like to recommend the following agenda for our meeting:

- Learn more about your organization and the key challenges you are facing, along with your important business objectives for the coming year
- Discuss what you need to do in order to gain advantage over your competition in the marketplace
- Learn about the role your key team members play in helping you achieve your objectives
- Discuss what is stopping you from achieving your stated objectives
- Provide you with a thumbnail overview of our experience and track record
- Discuss next steps, if we feel we should move forward from here

How does this sound to you? Is there anything you would like to add?"

Realizing that any tool or technique put to use by the counter-intuitive selling professional has a purpose behind it, let's take a closer look at the counter-intuitive call agenda in order to understand its objectives.

The underlying objectives of the counter-intuitive call agenda are to:

- demonstrate to a G.U.I.D.O. that you are not going to waste his or her time.
- provide a framework for the limited time that you have together.
- control the areas/topics that will be discussed.
- set the stage for the majority of the discussion to focus on the G.U.I.D.O, his or her organization, challenges, and people.
- offer the opportunity for the G.U.I.D.O. to add to the agenda.

Now let's examine each element of the counter-intuitive call agenda individually:

- Until you understand what is on G.U.I.D.O.'s mind (what keeps him or her up at night), you have no basis from which to offer any assistance. Focusing first on key challenges and objectives will provide you with the ammunition you need to help solve these critical issues.
- Beating the competition is usually a high priority for G.U.I.D.O.—if he or she runs an organization that faces competition. Asking about the competition gives you the insight you need in this area.
- Remember the "D" element of a G.U.I.D.O.'s makeup—delegation. G.U.I.D.O. gets things done through people, so understanding his or her view of key team members is *critical.*
- Only after you learn about G.U.I.D.O. and what is foremost in his or her mind at the current time should you offer any insight into your organization and how you can assist G.U.I.D.O. with pressing issues. When you do offer your "thumbnail overview" be sure to keep it short; less that five minutes is the goal. As a

guiding principle for your thumbnail overview, look to focus on sharing a success story or two about a customer that had similar issues and how you assisted them in their efforts. This will answer a question that is always foremost on a G.U.I.D.O.'s mind: **who else says so?**

- Agree up front to discuss the next steps, to plant the seed in G.U.I.D.O.'s mind that there will be next steps and that this meeting will be the beginning of a mutually beneficial long-term relationship.
- Provide the opportunity for G.U.I.D.O. to add to the agenda or alter it, so that—once agreement is reached—you've gained the "unwritten right" to pull the discussions back to the agreed-upon agenda if, for any reason, the conversations begin to stray.

Drawing Upon Your Team of Experts

There is also another element to the counter-intuitive call agenda that you can keep in your back pocket and bring out if and when you need to utilize it to conclude a meeting, while at the same time ensuring that you will reconvene with the G.U.I.D.O. within a short period of time.

Imagine that you are in a meeting with a G.U.I.D.O. when you begin to realize that you need to get some expert advice and guidance from other members of your team. In other words, you know that there is a solution that you can bring to G.U.I.D.O., only you may feel a little overwhelmed at the moment; or perhaps G.U.I.D.O. is getting into a subject area in which you do not have the expertise needed to create the best solution for the major issue he or she is describing to you.

At this point in your conversation, it is an ideal time to look at G.U.I.D.O. and say, "You've shared a lot of great information with me about your organization and where you feel you need to be. I recommend that I take this back to our team of experts for some recommendations and that we reconvene. Let's open our calendars and schedule the next meeting."

Hold this element of the counter-intuitive meeting agenda in reserve for specific situations that may arise. By utilizing it, you are dis-
playing to G.U.I.D.O. that you are a total and complete professional,
backed by a team of experts that assist you in crafting truly specialized
solutions for people just like G.U.I.D.O.

Playing "Doctor"

Using the counter-intuitive meeting agenda also assists both you
and G.U.I.D.O. in maintaining the mindset needed for success in
your initial meetings. This success will stay with you long after your
initial meetings as you grow and develop your relationship together.

Think of your role in your first meeting with G.U.I.D.O. as that of
a doctor and a patient; in this case you are the doctor and G.U.I.D.O.
is the patient. It is important that you maintain the **mindset of the
doctor** during the time you spend with G.U.I.D.O.

What would think if you walked into your doctor tomorrow and
he or she looked at you and said, "I think it's time we take your ap-
pendix out today"? What would you feel is wrong with this situation?

First of all, you would probably turn around and run out of your
doctor's office as fast as you could, thinking to yourself, "That's crazy!
How can he or she make that statement and recommendation when he
or she **hasn't even asked me any questions** or examined me?" Your next
step would probably be to contact another doctor for a second opinion.

As you work with a G.U.I.D.O. during your first face-to-face meeting, make sure you **examine the situation completely** before making
any recommendations or offering information about you and your
solutions. If you do not do this, anything you say will **become suspect**
to G.U.I.D.O., and he or she will **seek a second opinion**—from your
competition.

You'll learn more about dealing with the competition in the next
chapter. But for now, take a moment to complete The Successful
Seven from this chapter.

The Successful Seven: Chapter 29
Action Steps for Mastering the Art of Counter-Intuitive Selling

1. Use the **counter-intuitive meeting agenda** to provide a **framework and structure** for your initial meeting with a G.U.I.D.O.

2. Before moving past the agenda, be sure to gain G.U.I.D.O.'s agreement on the agenda. This provides you with the **"unwritten right" to bring the meeting back on track** to the agenda if it veers off course.

3. Remember that **less is more** when it comes to the amount of information that you share about you and your solutions during your first meeting with a G.U.I.D.O.

4. All of the information that G.U.I.D.O. shares with you during your initial face-to-face meeting should be gathered with one thought in mind: creating the perception in G.U.I.D.O.'s mind that you are an expert who will **only make recommendations after you fully understand** his or her situation and priorities.

5. Be sure to place emphasis on learning about **G.U.I.D.O.'s key people**. Remember that G.U.I.D.O. *delegates*. He or she gets things done through others.

6. Keep the "thumbnail overview" that you provide of yourself and your solutions to a bare minimum, and share it through **success stories** of how you have assisted others.

7. Keep yourself in the **mindset of a doctor** as you converse with a G.U.I.D.O. Ask a lot of questions and fully understand the current situation before you offer any recommendations.

chapter thirty

The Most Powerful Counter-Intuitive Selling Weapon: The Counter-Offensive

---

When the competition senses that you are winning the deal and
it is losing, it will begin to act in very predictable ways. By
launching your counter-intuitive offensive early, you will make
the competition's behavior appear *highly suspect*

Ken was sitting in Rich's office with him when Rich received a
phone call. He could tell by Rich's smile that one of Ken's competitors was on the other end of the line. Ken had been working with Rich
and his team at Transformation Software for about four months; the
company was either about to become one of Ken's major customers,
or a major customer of Ken's number one competitor. Although Ken
gestured to him and started to stand up to leave his office, Rich mo-
tioned for Ken to sit back down.

Ken could hear his competitor's voice coming through the re-
ceiver, beginning to tell Rich that he had great news to share. It appeared that his company had re-evaluated its proposal and based on
some "new findings" it would now be able to make some significant
price concessions, along with reducing service costs and cutting the
project time down as well. It all sounded too familiar, and Ken was
glad that he was finally on the other side and in control of the situation. Ken's competitor spoke with great excitement, obviously expecting Rich to say, "Great, when can you come in and talk about this in
more detail?"

Instead, Rich's response was short, sweet, and to the point. "This all sounds great, but no thanks. I think we're all set." Ken's competitor must have been taken by surprise, because the conversation ended quickly.

Rich hung up, looked at Ken, and said, "Very interesting. You told me that would happen. Now, where were we?"

The amazing thing is that, until this point, Rich had not shared with Ken that he had won the business. There were hints that Ken was leading all other contenders; that was as much knowledge as he'd had of Rich's decision.

It was becoming clear that launching his counter-offensive earlier, rather than later, had just paid a very large dividend. It all went back to a conversation Ken had with Rich about three weeks earlier.

Launching a Counter-Offensive

Ken was wrapping up a visit with Rich and the team involved in selecting the partner that would be awarded the very large, long-term contract with Transformation Software. It was close to the point where the team, with Rich leading, would begin to narrow the field. Although Ken knew he had a superior business solution for their needs, he wanted to make sure that he set the stage now for what he knew would begin to happen in the weeks to come.

Ken also wanted to make sure that he would not end up in a pricing battle with the other leading company in his market space—the "not so nice guys" that would go to any extreme in price concessions at the last minute to steal the deal. Quite frankly, Ken had heard the following one too many times from one too many prospects: "Ken, your solution was absolutely better, no doubt. But in the end, when your competitor came down in price and made the gap so wide, it was impossible for anyone here to justify the difference—even our CEO, and especially our CFO."

But now, Ken knew he had the right audience, and he appeared to be in the right position—leading in the value proposition of the solution and the demonstration of expertise to deliver. But he had to avoid the last-minute "price meltdown."

As they were about to conclude their latest meeting, Ken asked the team if there was anything else they needed to cover from their perspective. After moving through a few items and clearing the slate, he seized the opportunity.

"There is one more critical topic," Ken said, "and I'd like to make sure we cover it to your satisfaction."

"When my competitor begins to sense you might potentially award your business to my company, it is going to march back in here with all kinds of crazy offers and concessions, attempting to take your focus away from the real issues at hand. I realize from our discussions that you agree that we have the solution to address your real business issues and create significant value for your stakeholders, so I want to make sure that you will not be swayed or enticed by my competitor's last-minute panic tactics."

With that, Ken did the most critical and important thing he could possibly do. He shut up and focused on watching each of the team members for any and all of their reactions. They looked at each other and, without saying a word, simultaneously gave Rich the nod to speak for them.

"Ken, I appreciate your candor and concern. Rest assured that after all of the time we've invested in thoroughly understanding the options we have and the magnitude of the impact of our decision, we will not be swayed by the attempts of any company, including yours, to take the focus off of the decision criteria we have established."

It was time for Ken to insert the final counter-offensive statement into their thinking. "The other factor you may want to think about is this: if any company, including mine, would come in here and all of a sudden drastically reduce the cost to you, or tell you that it can somehow now complete the project in half the time, what does this say about the company's credibility? I just want you to ask yourself, if they could offer this now, why didn't they offer it up front?"

Rich smiled and said, "Good point, Ken. I appreciate you mentioning it to us."

Taking Control

What if Rich and his team had not responded in the way that they did? What if they started to stare at the floor (a telltale sign that you need to be critically concerned that the business will not be awarded to you) or began debating the information Ken had just shared?

Here is the beauty of the counter-intuitive counter-offensive. Regardless of the response from your prospect to your counter-offensive, when it is launched **early enough** in the sales process it provides you the opportunity to respond and, if needed, get your sales effort (and your prospect) back on track! However, be sure to never launch it until you have at least received **positive buying signs** from your prospect. These signs indicate that they:

- see the value in your solution,
- are satisfied with your demonstrated ability to deliver on your promise, and
- are nearing a point of either selecting the winner or narrowing the field of contenders.

Once you launch your counter-offensive, if your prospect responds the way that Rich and his team responded, then you have created a wall between yourself and any competitor that attempts to gain an advantage through additional price concessions, project descoping, or other "**panic tactics.**"

If, on the other hand, your prospect appears to waiver once you launch your counter-offensive, this is a clear warning sign that you have not done your job. You may have failed to demonstrate the value proposition for your solution along with your ability to deliver it, and/or you may have failed to create a dissatisfaction gap between your solution and anything a competitor can offer.

How do you find out where you missed the mark? The answer to this question is simpler than it may first appear. By setting the stage with your counter-intuitive counter-offensive, you have created the dynamics that allow you to simply ask where you might have fallen short in explaining the benefits of your solution. By doing so, you will find out everything you need to know to regain your prospect's confidence and regain the lead position.

There is no need to make this step any more complicated than it needs to be. If Rich had not responded as he did, Ken would have simply asked this question: "Rich, I sense that you and your team aren't convinced that our solution will best address your needs and create the stakeholder value you need from this investment. Could you and the team share with me where we missed the mark?"

This approach is short and to the point. By asking, you will learn what you need to cover and how you need to cover it. That's the great thing about customers and prospects: **they will tell us everything we need to know, if we just ask the right questions in the right way**.

Start preparing immediately to use your counter-offensive in all of your selling opportunities, and you will significantly increase your closing percentages. It's time to stop wondering how the competition stole that last deal from you. **Take control now**, and you'll be the one leaving the competition in the dust from this point forward in your selling career—not the other way around!

The Successful Seven: Chapter 30
Action Steps for Mastering the Art of Counter-Intuitive Selling

1. Get into the **habit of playing offense**, rather than defense, as you begin to master the art of counter-intuitive selling.

2. **Monitor your progress** through the sales cycle closely in order to launch your counter-offensive at the right time, rather than when it's too late.

3. Do not launch your counter-offensive **until you are sure** that your prospect:

   - sees value in your solution,

   - is satisfied with your demonstrated ability to deliver on your promise, and

   - indicates that they are nearing a point of either selecting a winner or narrowing the field of contenders.

4. If your prospect's response indicates agreement with your counter-offensive, then be sure to **share the "credibility factor" question** to give even more power to the counter-offensive.

5. If your prospect's response indicates any doubt about your counter-offensive, this is an indication that you need to **retrace the steps** of the sales cycle to determine where you missed the mark.

6. If the situation in number 5 comes into play, simply ask your prospect, **"Where did we miss the mark?"**

7. Once you learn what you need to do to regain the confidence and commitment of your prospect, be sure **to rally all of your resources** to deliver on the gap your prospect shares with you, and do so with a **sense of urgency!**

Leverage Yourself Through Multiple Impressions

Building your presence through top-of-mind awareness

chapter thirty-one

The Importance and
Power of Multiple Impressions

The building of your virtual relationship with G.U.I.D.O. and others is a continuous journey, just like your journey into the world of counter-intuitive selling. Use opportunities wisely as you build awareness and familiarity.

Ken was wrapping up a successful first meeting with a major G.U.I.D.O. that he had been pursuing for over 18 months. Although it had been a long road to today's meeting, Ken was feeling that it had now been well worth the effort.

The effort had not been a full-time endeavor. Ken had carefully kept this G.U.I.D.O. on his radar screen, making occasional calls into the G.U.I.D.O.'s assistant, and, perhaps even more importantly, continuing to send counter-intuitive intelligence across G.U.I.D.O.'s desk.

As the meeting was concluding, Ken asked the G.U.I.D.O., "Is there anything else we need to cover today?"

When G.U.I.D.O. responded that there was nothing else from his end, Ken took the opportunity to pose the question that he always does when he finally lands the first appointment with a high-potential G.U.I.D.O.

"Then I have one question for you: what was it that sparked you to set our meeting for today—to actually put it into your calendar and keep it there?"

"It was your call a few weeks ago," G.U.I.D.O. responded. "The brief conversation that we had peaked my interest."

Although the average sales professional would be satisfied with this answer—if he or she even thought to pose the question—Ken knew it was time to dig deeper.

"Besides our very brief conversation a few weeks ago, what else prompted you to agree to meet? I imagine that there is more."

G.U.I.D.O. thought for a few minutes, retracing his steps, and then replied, "Actually, Ken, there was the invitation you sent me to the executive roundtable a few months back. It was something that I wanted to attend, but it was right during our analyst meetings and our earnings call. I just couldn't fit it in. The topic, however, seemed to be right on target with what we discussed today."

Even though Ken found G.U.I.D.O.'s response extremely revealing, he had a hunch that there was more. "The good news about the executive roundtable is that because it was such a success, and because there is more to share on the topic than we were able to cover, we are just about to schedule the next one. I'll be sure to let you know as soon as the date is solid, and I'll give you a call even before the invitations are extended."

"I appreciate that, Ken, I really do," G.U.I.D.O. said, with a nod of thanks.

"Was there anything else that prompted you to finally decide we needed to meet?" Ken asked.

After again thinking about it, G.U.I.D.O. had more to share. "Actually, Ken, come to think of it, there was the case study that you sent with one of your letters. I circulated that to the rest of my executive team. I received a number of unsolicited positive comments about it at the time, but the timing just wasn't right to delve into the issue any deeper."

"I appreciate your insight," Ken responded. "It is very helpful to me. I look forward to our next meeting. As you suggested, I'll coordinate our schedules with Alice on my way out, and I'll let her know the others that you want to be available to join us. I'll make sure it is all taken care of."

"Thanks, Ken." G.U.I.D.O. rose to head to his next meeting—the one for which Alice had just called to remind him that he was running late. "I appreciate your taking the lead on this, as I'm afraid I will let it fall through the cracks, which is not what I want to do right now. I'll see you again in a few weeks."

Building Familiarity Through Multiple Impressions

Ken was becoming a master at the art of building virtual relationships with G.U.I.D.O.s, and he was also learning that this element of counter-intuitive selling also worked just as well when it came to establishing virtual relationships—and not so virtual relationships—with H.A.N.K.s and H.E.R.B.s.

Over the past 18 months, after attempting to reach this G.U.I.D.O. through a counter-intuitive letter campaign and not realizing success, Ken decided to extend his campaign through the use of periodic pieces of counter-intuitive intelligence. He made sure that one of these crossed G.U.I.D.O.'s desk on a somewhat random, but yet repetitive, schedule.

Ken's goal was simple: continue to place his name and his presence in front of G.U.I.D.O. in order to build familiarity and awareness.

How did Ken do this?

Ken leveraged many sources and events to create a continual and periodic stream of counter-intuitive intelligence crossing G.U.I.D.O.'s desk. These pieces of counter-intuitive intelligence could arrive through the mail, overnight deliveries, e-mail, or voice-mail messages.

It was very important that anything Ken used as a vehicle to build his relationship with G.U.I.D.O. fit very specific criteria. Ken was very careful to make sure that each and every piece of counter-intuitive intelligence he used was of potential value, and that none of it could run the risk of being viewed as useless by G.U.I.D.O.

Each time Ken put a piece of counter-intuitive intelligence to work in building a relationship with G.U.I.D.O. he made sure that he personalized it by including a handwritten note, highlighting an article or case study, or calling or e-mailing G.U.I.D.O. to give him a "heads up" that something was on its way.

Using Counter-Intuitive Intelligence

Over the course of the preceding 18 months, Ken had incorporated the following counter-intuitive intelligence into his campaign with G.U.I.D.O:

- White papers
- Research reports
- Invitations to executive briefings and roundtables
- Article reprints
- Analyst research
- Interviews
- Case studies
- Technical reviews
- *Wall Street Journal* articles
- Testimonial letters

For example, when Ken found a timely article or research report that he believed would be helpful to G.U.I.D.O., he would print a high-quality copy, highlight some key points, put it into an overnight envelope, and send it off. The most critical component of this counter-intuitive intelligence was the *handwritten note* that Ken attached to each and every piece before sending it to G.U.I.D.O.

For example, one of Ken's notes to G.U.I.D.O., written on very expensive-looking, small (usually no larger than 8-by-5½ inches) stationery with "From the Desk of Ken Sellit" printed at the top, might read something like this:

> [G.U.I.D.O.'s name]—
>
> As I read this, I thought it might be of interest to you and helpful to you and your team. A number of my clients are finding this an important area of focus to improve results.
>
> See page 4, as I highlighted a few of what I found to be the most salient points.
>
> Best personal regards,
>
> Ken

As you closely examine this counter-intuitive note from **Ken** to G.U.I.D.O., be sure to take special note as to what is missing. What you will *not* find on the note are any of the following:

- The name of Ken's company
- Ken's phone number
- The address of Ken's company
- Ken's e-mail address

By design, Ken makes sure that all of this information is **omitted**.

Why?

The answer is quite simple: eliminating this information is counter-intuitive. Most salespeople would include that information on any written communication with a prospect, and G.U.I.D.O. certainly expects to see that information on a note attached to something that is sent to him from a salesperson.

In today's world of in-your-face marketing and selling, this approach is something that G.U.I.D.O. appreciates. As he opens the envelope and sees the document with a simple, short, handwritten and personalized note attached to it, he probably thinks to himself, "How refreshing. Here's something that might just be helpful, and it's not attached to the fact that someone is trying to sell me something."

Actually, Ken *is* trying to sell G.U.I.D.O. something; he's just being a little **counter-intuitive** about it! You will learn more counter-intuitive techniques for communicating with G.U.I.D.O. in the next chapter; but now, take a moment to commit to The Successful Seven for this chapter.

The Successful Seven: Chapter 31
Action Steps for Mastering the Art of Counter-Intuitive Selling

1. Improve your **awareness and familiarity** with G.U.I.D.O.s (it also works just as well with H.A.N.K.s and H.E.R.B.s) through the use of a campaign of counter-intuitive intelligence.

2. Get your counter-intuitive intelligence in front of G.U.I.D.O. on a **random but periodic basis.**

3. Make sure that anything you use as counter-intuitive intelligence has **relevance and importance** to G.U.I.D.O.

4. Always attach a **handwritten note** to the counter-intuitive intelligence that you send to a G.U.I.D.O. Use very **high-quality** paper for these notes.

5. Sign **only your name** to the handwritten notes you attach to your counter-intuitive intelligence. By design, do not include your contact information.

6. **Vary the delivery vehicle** for your counter-intuitive intelligence: use overnight delivery, Priority Mail, e-mail, voicemail, and more.

7. Realize that it **takes multiple impressions** to reach into a G.U.I.D.O.'s mind, and that you may never know which impression actually caused G.U.I.D.O. to take action and meet with you—but be sure to ask and see what you can learn.

chapter thirty-two

PowerNotes: Being First

Counter-Intuitive *PowerNotes* are an important step in building
virtual relationships, and they can make you appear larger than
life when meeting with members of G.U.I.D.O.'s team.

The counter-intuitive PowerNote is a personalized, hand-written
note to a key contact that has several very important and unique characteristics:

- It helps you gain mindshare with the individual it is sent to.
- It is designed to begin to establish credibility with the recipient
  by not looking or sounding like a sales letter (it has the appear-
  ance on the outside of a fancy, personalized invitation).
- It establishes that you are looking to create value for the
  recipient.
- It is designed to leave the recipient intrigued by its uniqueness.
- It is short—no more than 4 or 5 sentences at the most.

Leverage the Moment with PowerNotes

When Ken secured an appointment with a trusted H.A.N.K. inside one of his target high-potential prospects, he figured it was a
good event to leverage into a PowerNote to G.U.I.D.O. Ken had
learned enough about H.A.N.K. to know that he was highly respected
by G.U.I.D.O.

Why was this an important time for a PowerNote to G.U.I.D.O.?

During his journey into the world of counter-intuitive selling, Ken was quickly appreciating the value and urgency of building his **virtual relationship** with G.U.I.D.O. Without establishing the virtual relationship first, it would be much more difficult to establish the face-to-face relationship he would eventually need in order to be as successful as possible in doing business with G.U.I.D.O. and his organization.

Beginning a Virtual Relationship with PowerNotes.

When Ken returned to his office, he immediately sat down to write his follow-up note to H.A.N.K. Ken had always sent follow-up notes, and it had always paid large dividends. What he never thought about until he entered the world of counter-intuitive selling was the dual importance of also **sending a PowerNote to G.U.I.D.O. after meeting with anyone** from G.U.I.D.O.'s organization.

Ken sat down and penned his PowerNote to G.U.I.D.O. His PowerNotes always went onto very expensive-looking note cards with "Ken Sellit" engraved across the top. The envelopes matched the parchment paper of the note card. The only information on the envelope was Ken's home address, which was engraved as well, in very small print on the back side of the envelope.

Ken's PowerNote had the look and feel of a very expensive, handwritten invitation, so it was often left unopened by G.U.I.D.O.'s assistant. Most of the time, G.U.I.D.O. would personally unseal the envelope. If G.U.I.D.O.'s assistant did open the PowerNote, it would be left on the top of the pile of mail for G.U.I.D.O. Either way, its look, feel, and mysterious nature earned it top priority status—**along with high visibility**.

Ken's PowerNote read something like this:

> [G.U.I.D.O.'s name]—
>
> I had the opportunity to meet with [H.A.N.K.'s name] today. Her insight into your current objectives and the challenges you face in meeting these objectives will prove invaluable moving forward. We are planning to meet again once I review some of the information. Early indications are that we may be able to provide some expertise to accelerate your ability to meet the goals you have set for the organization. If there is a decision to move forward, you have my personal commitment to deliver the results you expect from a quality partnership. I will keep you updated on our discussions.
>
> Best personal regards,
>
> Ken Sellit

Because the purpose of Ken's PowerNote is different than the purpose of the counter-intuitive intelligence that he sends to G.U.I.D.O., Ken always includes a business card along with his Power-Note. The difference is simple: you want to make sure that G.U.I.D.O. has the information he needs in case he wants to reach out to you as a result of your PowerNote. You'll learn more about how to create your own counter-intuitive business card in Chapter 35, but for now, just realize that you do not include your existing business card inside your PowerNote.

Ken's PowerNotes have several very important objectives that set them apart from other notes, including:

- **Creating awareness** with G.U.I.D.O. that Ken is in discussions with a key member of his team.
- **Creating counter-intuitive intrigue**, by not asking for anything from G.U.I.D.O. (remember, normal salespeople "pound from the outside" while the counter-intuitive selling professional seeks to have G.U.I.D.O. "reach out from the inside").

- Opening up **direct lines of communication** with G.U.I.D.O.
- Creating a **safety valve** in case the discussions with H.A.N.K. do not go as anticipated.
- Enabling Ken to say to H.A.N.K., **"I've communicated with him,"** if H.A.N.K. asks whether Ken knows G.U.I.D.O.
- Creating **another impression** along the counter-intuitive journey of connecting with G.U.I.D.O.
- Potentially **acting as a catalyst** for G.U.I.D.O. to ask H.A.N.K., "How did your meeting go with Ken Sellit?"

As you can see, although the PowerNote is a small and quick counter-intuitive selling tool, it certainly has a lot of value and can deliver high-potential rewards as your journey continues.

PowerNotes also work just as well when sent to H.A.N.K.s or H.E.R.B.s. Once you identify a H.A.N.K. or a H.E.R.B. and you are attempting to secure time on his or her calendar without success, a PowerNote will often do the trick. Although H.A.N.K. and H.E.R.B. are typically easier to reach than G.U.I.D.O., there are situations in which H.A.N.K and H.E.R.B. can be challenging to nail down.

This often occurs when a H.E.R.B. is on the fast track to become a G.U.I.D.O. or when a very high-profile initiative places H.E.R.B. in the spotlight and under the gun to produce results in a very short period of time. Regardless of the reason, if you are having a difficult time reaching a H.A.N.K. or a H.E.R.B., a PowerNote can be extremely effective in getting his or her attention and getting a response.

There is also a somewhat subliminal benefit that you gain when you begin to use PowerNotes effectively in your communications with G.U.I.D.O. After receiving your PowerNote and looking at your card and the message, G.U.I.D.O. starts to think to himself, "Who is this?" Through your PowerNote you have increased awareness and created intrigue. You've taken the first step in building your virtual relationship with G.U.I.D.O.

Leveraging G.U.I.D.O.'s Knowledge and Influence

PowerNotes can also be extremely effective in leveraging one G.U.I.D.O. to help create awareness with another. Once you begin to establish your relationships with G.U.I.D.O.s, and especially if you begin to take community involvement seriously, you will often find yourself in conversation with a G.U.I.D.O. who knows other G.U.I.D.O.s. The name of another G.U.I.D.O. might come up, or you might ask about a specific G.U.I.D.O., to see if the two indeed know each other and whether one can help you gain insight about another.

In either case, this is also a great opportunity to put your Power-Notes into action. Ken now does this quite often, and one of his recent PowerNotes read something like this:

> [G.U.I.D.O.'s name]—
>
> I was having a conversation with [G.U.I.D.O. "A"] last week, when your name came up in conversation. During our discussion, [G.U.I.D.O. "A"] suggested that I reach out to you to discuss some of the initiatives we are currently considering with [G.U.I.D.O. "A"]'s team. I am curious to receive your thoughts and advice on whether your organization is wresting with similar issues. I will call JoAnn to schedule a few minutes for us to talk or possibly get together, as I am often near your office visiting with [G.U.I.D.O. "A"] and members of his team. I look forward to our dialog.
>
> Best personal regards,
>
> Ken Sellit

In both situations—using PowerNotes to reach out to a G.U.I.D.O. after meeting with a member of his team and using Pow-erNotes to reach out to another G.U.I.D.O—your PowerNotes are an effective counter-intuitive tool.

Once again, you'll have a G.U.I.D.O. asking himself, "Who is this?" And remember, awareness is half the battle.

The Successful Seven: Chapter 32
Action Steps for Mastering the Art of Counter-Intuitive Selling

1. Utilize PowerNotes to establish your virtual relationship with a G.U.I.D.O. early—as soon as you meet with any member of the G.U.I.D.O.'s team.

2. Make sure your PowerNotes carry an expensive look and feel. Use engraved notes, with only your name engraved on the note itself and only your home address engraved onto the back of the envelope.

3. Include a business card (or two) inside of your PowerNote. Do not use your normal business cards; use your counter-intuitive business cards (you'll learn about these in Chapter 35).

4. Use your PowerNotes to open up a channel of direct communication with a G.U.I.D.O., and to act as a safety value in case discussions with your other contacts do not go as planned.

5. PowerNotes are also an effective counter-intuitive tool when you are experiencing challenges in reaching a high-profile H.A.N.K or H.E.R.B.

6. Use your PowerNotes to leverage your contact with one G.U.I.D.O. into the opportunity to contact another G.U.I.D.O.

7. Use your PowerNotes effectively to build awareness and familiarity with G.U.I.D.O.s.

chapter thirty-three

You Always Have a Packed Calendar—Even If Tomorrow Is Wide Open

---

No matter what is on your calendar for the next few weeks, you are busy with a packed calendar. Successful people are busy people; this is the other impression you need to create with G.U.I.D.O.s.

Ken cringed as he listened to the newest member of the sales team, Bob, on the phone working to fill his appointment book. As Ken listened, he thought to himself, "No wonder Bob's calendar is wide open. If I received a call and heard Bob on the other end of the phone, I wouldn't agree to meet with him either."

It was obvious that Bob was not yet a student of counter-intuitive selling. His delivery sounded like that of most salespeople *before* mastering the art of the unexpected: "Hello. My name is Bob Campbell and I am with Star National Systems. We sell customized resource planning systems and I would like to set up a time to come see you to sell you one of these for your company. Is it possible that you could find an hour or so on your schedule when I can come and meet with you so I can tell you all about our system?"

What Bob did next was worse than this opening pitch, and it destroyed his chances of ever establishing any credibility with the G.U.I.D.O.

Ken continued to listen as Bob got further into the conversation. From the sound of one of Bob's responses, Ken recognized what question had been asked by the person on the other end of the phone. He suspected that the prospect had asked, "When are you available to come out here and meet with me?"

Bob responded, "I'm available anytime. I don't have anything on my calendar at the moment. You name the date and time! How about tomorrow morning, first thing, say around 11:00?"

At this point, Ken imagined that the individual on the other end of the phone must have been thinking, "What am I getting myself into now? This guy sounds so excited, I must be the first one to ever give him an appointment. After all, he just told me his calendar is wide open!"

Ken waited for Bob to wrap up the call—which seemed to take forever—and then he turned to Bob and said, "Bob, what was that all about?"

Bob responded, "That was awesome. I just landed an appointment with one of the big guys over at McLindsey and Company. Sounds like they need what we have to offer. I'm seeing him first thing tomorrow, around 11:00."

Listening to Bob's response, Ken just smiled to himself, realizing that Bob was in for a real education when he started learning about counter-intuitive selling. Ken knew, however, that one critical piece of advice could not wait any longer, so he looked at Bob and offered some counseling.

"Bob, let me just give you one word of advice right now," Ken said. "Even when there is absolutely nothing on your calendar for tomorrow, the next day, or even further out, **your schedule is jam-packed**. Got it? When you get to the point in the conversation with your prospect when you need to nail down the appointment, you need to let the person know that there are a few small windows of time that are available for you to see them. It's that simple."

Looking a little confused, Bob responded, "But what if I have a wide-open schedule? What do I do then?"

Ken tried to drive the point home one more time. "Bob, you're booked—solid. End of story. You need to get into a counter-intuitive mindset about this."

Ken could see that perhaps it was not yet that simple—at least not to Bob. Bob needed to understand the mindset of the counter-intuitive selling professional in order to understand the simplicity of what Ken was attempting to share with him.

Remember that Successful People Want to Deal with Other Successful People

As Bob learns more about the art of the unexpected, he will learn one of the most important guiding principles and traits of the counter-intuitive selling professional:

> Successful people like to deal with other successful people. Successful people are busy people; therefore, they expect to deal with other busy people. A successful person's calendar is always full, no matter what is really on the calendar.

In Chapter 19, we discussed the importance of being on equal footing with a G.U.I.D.O. An aspect of this equal footing is the fact that you are both successful, busy individuals, and that your time is extremely limited. As you deal with more and more G.U.I.D.O.s, you will quickly realize that their calendars are always full.

At the same time, you also need to realize the other equally important fact about a G.U.I.D.O.'s calendar: if something becomes important enough, it will find its way onto G.U.I.D.O.'s calendar. It's that simple!

Here is the challenge for the sales professional entering the world of counter-intuitive selling: how do you get to the point in your career where your calendar is booked, except for limited available times into which you can insert important meetings?

The answer is simple: you create it. You create it today by filling out your calendar for the next week or two weeks. You immediately start telling the people that you call, "I don't have anything available on my calendar for the next two weeks. I am really jam packed. The first thing I have available is a week from next Tuesday. What do you have available that day? Let's see if we can get something to work."

All of a sudden, as you can imagine, the person on the other end of the phone begins to think, "Wow, he really is busy! He's got nothing available for over two weeks. I'd better get on his calendar now, even if I have to move a few things around."

Never Underestimate the Importance of a G.U.I.D.O.'s Assistant

This technique is especially effective when you are dealing with a G.U.I.D.O.'s assistant. Remember, the primary role of G.U.I.D.O.'s assistant is to manage and maximize G.U.I.D.O.'s calendar, and there are several things that are true about a G.U.I.D.O.'s calendar:

- There is never enough time for all of the items that need to be on G.U.I.D.O.'s calendar.
- G.U.I.D.O. is always asking his or her assistant to fit more into the calendar—even when there is no more time to fill!
- Last-minute calendar and schedule changes are a fact of life for G.U.I.D.O. and his or her assistant.
- Certain events take priority and knock other appointments off of a G.U.I.D.O.'s calendar. These include a call from the chairman or a board member, customer issues, unexpected board meetings, emergencies (personal and career), and being suddenly called out of town, just to name a few.

Here's an even more important aspect to remember: a G.U.I.D.O.'s assistant is an expert at juggling G.U.I.D.O.'s calendar. He or she has the unique ability to—in the end—make the calendar work and to get scheduled what needs to get scheduled. That ability is one of the reasons that G.U.I.D.O. hired the person in the first place.

When you call a G.U.I.D.O.'s assistant to get on the calendar or when he or she calls you to rearrange your meeting, remember that this is the assistant's area of expertise, and he or she will appreciate your flexibility and understanding when there is a need to reschedule your appointment with G.U.I.D.O.

This is also a great time in our journey to talk about just how important a G.U.I.D.O.'s assistant is to you as a counter-intuitive selling professional. As you master the art of the unexpected, you will begin to notice something very powerful: **more than 50 percent of the time, you will get onto a G.U.I.D.O.'s calendar without ever talking to G.U.I.D.O.**

G.U.I.D.O.'s assistant is *vital* to the counter-intuitive selling professional because he or she:

- Completely controls G.U.I.D.O.'s calendar and time.
- Decides who gets onto the calendar.
- Decides what will come off of the calendar when something more critical takes precedent.
- Determines how much time something or someone gets with G.U.I.D.O.
- Understands G.U.I.D.O. and his thinking about who he or she will or will not see.
- Influences G.U.I.D.O. and his thinking about who he or she will or will not see.
- Appreciates your flexibility and patience when the schedule needs to be rearranged.
- Remembers the individuals who display respect and kindness at all times.
- Can, if needed, block your access to G.U.I.D.O.

Just in case the importance of a G.U.I.D.O.'s assistant in your pursuit and eventual meeting with G.U.I.D.O. is not crystal clear at this point, perhaps this example will drive the point home. It is not uncommon, when the counter-intuitive selling professional meets with a G.U.I.D.O. for the first time, for G.U.I.D.O. to comment, "Ken, it is good to finally meet you. Judy said good things about you. Now, where should we start today?"

Enjoying the Power of a Packed Calendar

Before we conclude this chapter in your journey, let's get back to the importance of always having a packed schedule. Keeping a packed schedule is like any new habit that you are striving to master: it will take practice, it will take repetition, and it will take hard work. If you are ready to put in the effort, it will be well worth the energy for a number of reasons.

First of all, you will feel more successful when your calendar is full. You will feel "in demand" and that what you have to offer in the marketplace is producing results. You will also begin to feel that you can be more selective about who gets on your calendar—just like a G.U.I.D.O. This will also help you feel that you are on equal footing with G.U.I.D.O.s.

In addition, your mental attitude when you are on the phone setting appointments will be greatly improved and energized. There is nothing more powerful than saying to a G.U.I.D.O., "My schedule is jammed for a good two weeks out, as I imagine yours is, so let's look about three weeks out. Are you in town then? I have a few limited times available that could possibly work. Perhaps we both need to rearrange a few things to find a time that is good for both of us."

By now, you are probably thinking to yourself, "OK, I get it now, so how do I 'create' my packed schedule, and how do I do it right now?"

The answer may be easier than you expect it to be: *fill your calendar.*

There are plenty of activities and appointments, especially this early in your journey into the word of counter-intuitive selling, on which you can spend valuable time:

- Increase your schedule of I-Team appointments to take advantage of more time-spaced repetition practice needed to continue to improve your counter-intuitive selling skills.
- Schedule appointments with your key customers, and spend the time enhancing the success stories that you can use when holding your first face-to-face meetings with your target G.U.I.D.O.s.
- Spend scheduled time uncovering a new H.E.R.B. or H.A.N.K. inside your target prospects and key customers.
- Schedule time with your key mentors, share where you are in your counter-intuitive selling journey, and ask for feedback and advice.
- Block out time to build and refine your counter-intuitive letter campaigns.
- Create additional behavioral triggers that will accelerate your adoption of new habits and increase your success in the new world of counter-intuitive selling.

As you fill your calendar with these activities over the next few weeks, also begin to fill your calendar beyond two weeks with G.U.I.D.O. meetings, H.A.N.K./H.E.R.B. meetings, and scheduled time for your counter-intuitive campaigns and follow-up calls.

Remember, there is no other feeling in the world of counter-intuitive selling that compares to the moment when you can look at your calendar and say to yourself, "This is great, I am booked solid for the next two-and-a-half weeks. It's time to get started on filling the following week!"

You will feel differently about yourself and your success, and others will feel it as well.

The Successful Seven: Chapter 33
Action Steps for Mastering the Art of Counter-Intuitive Selling

1. Always have the counter-intuitive mindset that **your schedule is packed** over the next few weeks—regardless of what is on your calendar.

2. **Immediately create a booked calendar** by scheduling critical and essential activities over the next few weeks, including additional I-Team appointments that you will use to perfect your counter-intuitive selling skills.

3. When you are working to set appointments with a G.U.I.D.O. and his or her assistant, create the awareness that **your calendar is just as full as G.U.I.D.O.'s.**

4. Realize that a G.U.I.D.O.'s assistant is **an expert at managing and maximizing** G.U.I.D.O.'s calendar, and put this to work for you!

5. Realize that in the world of counter-intuitive selling, you will get onto a G.U.I.D.O.'s calendar **50 percent of the time without ever talking** to G.U.I.D.O.

6. Once your calendar is full, **make a personal commitment** to keep it full. Gauge the time you need to keep it full, and set additional, daily I-Team appointments designated specifically to appointment setting time to keep your calendar as booked as possible.

7. Use "**the power of a packed calendar**" to improve your energy level and your passion for what you do. You are busy and you are in demand, and this is fun!

chapter thirty-four

Learning a Lot by Saying Little

As the counter-intuitive selling professional begins to truly
master the art of the unexpected, he or she learns that clarifying
questions bring home important answers. It's all part of
creating the impression that you are a true professional.

One of the most critical traits of counter-intuitive selling that Ken
was still learning to master was the art of asking **short, clarifying questions** of his customer or prospect. It was a skill that he had been working on since his early mentoring days with Frank, and yet, it was still
hard for Ken to implement on a daily basis.

Ken had often talked to Frank about his challenge. "Why," Ken
would ask, "is this such a difficult skill to master? It sounds like it
should be easy. We should just keep quiet after we ask a short question
requesting clarity, and listen for the answer."

Frank would respond, "You see, Ken, that's why it is so difficult to
master. Salespeople like to hear themselves talk. You and I have talked
about this before. We hate the silence that comes after we ask a question. If we even get to the point where we are effective at asking questions for clarity, we can't disciple ourselves to wait through the
silence—which seems like it lasts forever—until the prospect or customer tells us exactly what we need to know. And that's the key, if we
learn how to do this effectively, **the customer will tell us everything we
need to know!**"

Learning to Use Clarifying Questions

While all of this made perfect sense to Ken, it was still very hard to put into practice. Ken realized that the key time to use clarifying questions was right after the customer or prospect poses a question or raises an objection, and also right after he or she states the reason for raising the objection.

Clarifying questions have one single objective: to get to the real reasons a customer or prospect is hesitant to move forward.

Ken made a personal commitment, right then and there, to continue to practice the art of posing clarifying questions until he had it mastered.

He decided that he would immediately create a behavioral trigger to place on his laptop screen, on the rearview mirror of his car, and on his desk in the office. The trigger would remind him to keep practicing his new behavior until it was a learned behavior that he did not even need to think about—it would just happen automatically.

Here is the behavioral trigger that Ken created:

> **ask**
> **clarify**
> **be silent**
> **listen**

The Follow-Up

Although Ken was still struggling with the art of asking clarifying questions, he had learned the power of the words that should follow any clarifying question that he posed to a prospect or customer. Right after an individual answers Ken's question—and especially when they do not offer an answer with a lot of detail—Ken asks the follow-up question, **"Can you tell me what you mean by that?"**

Ken learned this skill the hard way. Much too often, we take the first answer that a customer or prospect offers and we believe it is *the* answer. Not only that, **we think we** *understand* **what the customer or prospect** *meant*.

Ken recalls exactly when he learned this lesson. He had asked a customer a question about their impression of Ken's solution, and the prospect said to him, "Sounds like a great solution, but it's too expensive." After a little more conversation with the prospect, Ken realized that he was not in the position to lower his price. He thanked the individual for their time, and then departed. He truly believed he understood the prospect completely.

A few weeks later, while Ken was conducting routine follow-up calls to all of the prospects he had met with over the past month, he called this prospect to see if anything had changed with their situation. As it turned out, things had certainly changed.

When he asked the prospect how things were going, the prospect said, "Things are just great, thanks for asking. As a matter of fact, we went with one of your competitors and things are going just great. As you know, we really needed to implement something, and a few weeks after we met with you, we were able to free up some money and move forward. Thanks again for coming out to see us. We learned a lot from meeting with you."

Beside himself after hearing this from the prospect, Ken responded, "So I guess my competitor's price was considerably lower than mine, because you told me that what I proposed was too expensive."

What Ken heard next made him want to shrink into his chair and disappear.

"No, not at all. In fact, your competitor's solution was quite a bit more expensive. See, when I said that your solution was too expensive, what I meant was that we had no money in the budget for that quarter, so anything was too expensive at the time. Once we figured out how to free up the money a few weeks later, we were ready to get moving. So, thanks again for your time and the knowledge you provided to us."

Ken has never forgotten that lesson. As a result, he has become an expert in asking, "Can you share with me what you mean when you say that what I am proposing is too expensive?" Once he asks, he waits in silence until he hears the response. He does not say a word until the prospect speaks first. It all goes back to becoming a true counter-intuitive selling professional and being as thorough in your investigative work as a doctor. Probe for the real answers behind the initial answers, and get all of the information before you even being to think about the prescription for treating the symptoms.

This realization came as a revelation to Ken and prompted him to create the first behavioral trigger that he had ever used. He carries that trigger with him today and it has helped make him become more successful at asking follow-up questions for clarity. The behavioral trigger reads:

CLARITY
ASK:
What do you mean by...?

Carry Your Clarifying Questions with You

Today, Ken realizes just how much value he has gained—and how much money he has earned—as a result of putting that behavioral trigger to work on a daily basis. The great news is that he no longer needs it. Asking follow-up questions for clarity has become a learned habit.

Ken, however, knows that he still needs to improve his use of other clarifying questions, so he has built a list to carry with him in his Day-Timer. His list looks something like this:

Clarifying Questions: Ask these questions of the customer after he or she shares an objection or makes a statement. *DO NOT* accept the first answer that you hear!

- "Can you tell me what you mean by what you just shared?"
- "What do you mean when you say '(repeat back exactly what the customer just said)'?"
- "Tell me more…"
- "Hmm, that's interesting . . . what else can you tell me?"
- "What does that mean to you?"
- "Is there more you'd like to share?"

Ken laminated the list, and carries it with him at all times. Whenever he is face to face or on the phone with a prospect or customer, this list is right in front of him. This list, combined with Ken's "ask/clarify/be silent/listen" trigger form the complete behavior-changing regimen that he follows as his map for success. He knows that to change his behavior on a permanent basis, he needs to continue to use his behavioral triggers; Ken's committed to doing what it takes.

The Successful Seven: Chapter 34
Action Steps for Mastering the Art of Counter-Intuitive Selling

1. Commit to mastering the art of **asking clarifying questions**.

2. Use **behavioral triggers** to drive needed changes in your learned habits.

3. Practice the hard-to-master **skill of remaining silent** once you ask a clarifying question of the prospect or customer.

4. Never **assume that you understand** what a prospect or customer shares with you in his or her first response or that you **understand what they mean** when posing an initial objection.

5. Use clarifying questions to **achieve clarity** from your prospects and customers.

6. After every response from a prospect or customer, and after an objection has been raised, always ask, "**Can you tell me what you mean by what you just shared with me?**"

7. Create a **list of clarifying questions** to carry with you at all times. Keep it in front of you during all meetings and phone calls. Use it to drive your needed behavioral change.

part five

Putting It All Together

Remove Any Barriers to Becoming Their Equal

Breaking down any remaining walls

chapter thirty-five

Enter the "No Title World" That You Create

Titles create boundaries and limitations, and also limit the way we think and communicate. Remove titles from your business cards to expand your thinking—and the way your prospects and customers think about you. The counter-intuitive world is a world without titles.

In the world of counter-intuitive selling, perception is everything. As you work hard to gain equal footing with G.U.I.D.O.s and build relationships with H.A.N.K.s and H.E.R.B.s (who can help lead you to G.U.I.D.O.s), it is critical that you remove any and all barriers that can potentially hinder your efforts.

Titles are one of those barriers that must be removed—both from your mindset and from your business cards.

Let's think about the age-old practice of titles and, even more specifically, placing titles on business cards. What purpose does a title on a business card serve for you in the world of counter-intuitive selling? When your goal is to *not* appear as most salespeople appear, and to be perceived as someone who is *not* working to "sell" something to a G.U.I.D.O. and his team, then why in the world would you put a title such as "sales representative" on your business card?

When you begin to think about the world of titles that exists for salespeople, you begin to see the humor and paradox within the exercise.

When someone gets promoted within the world of sales, he or she may get a new title, such as senior sales representative. What does this title mean? Does it mean that the individual is now better at trying to sell something to his or her customers? What about the title of sales executive or account executive, the most common titles in the world of selling? What do these titles mean?

Let's take a close look at the impact your current business card might have in the world of counter-intuitive selling.

Being More Than Just the "Sales Guy"

Perhaps you have been working on a high-potential target prospect over the past few months. You have successfully launched a counter-intuitive letter campaign to an identified G.U.I.D.O. While doing so, you've also gathered your counter-intuitive intelligence through several H.E.R.B.s and H.A.N.K.s.

During an internal meeting, H.A.N.K. strikes up a conversation with G.U.I.D.O., and mentions you and your solution as something that should be considered for a major initiative that is high on G.U.I.D.O.'s priority list. H.A.N.K. hands G.U.I.D.O. your business card. Although G.U.I.D.O. does not yet make the connection between this business card and the letters he is receiving from you, he looks at the card, sees your title, and says to H.A.N.K., "If you think the solution is really something we should consider, let's make sure we're talking to more than the sales guy."

Ouch!

You are much more than the "sales guy," so it is time to remove these career-limiting titles from your business cards. If you are compelled to have a title, then get creative. Call yourself the "chief customer evangelist" or "solution specialist"—anything other than a sales rep. At a minimum, remove the word *sales* from your title on your business card. If you are a regional sales director today, become a regional director tomorrow. Get rid of the "sales" within your title right now!

Creating a Counter-Intuitive Business Card

What should your counter-intuitive business card look like, and what information should be on it? You must think about what every word on your business card means to your customers and prospects.

Your counter-intuitive business card should include only the following four items on its face:

1. Your name
2. Your company name
3. How to reach you by phone
4. How to reach you by e-mail

Notice what's missing?

The front of your counter-intuitive business card should be as clutter free and easy to read as possible. Why list more than one phone number? Listing more than one number only causes confusion. Only list the number where you can always be reached. List the number that travels with you—your mobile number. Remove all other numbers from your business card.

Why list your address? Why does it matter? Is G.U.I.D.O going to pick up your business card and say, "Let's go pay him a visit?"

How about a fax number? If G.U.I.D.O. needs your fax number to send the purchase order over to you, you'll want to know about it, so you can personally give him the number when he needs it. In today's world of counter-intuitive selling, fax numbers serve no purpose on your business card.

If you feel compelled to include a fax number, list an e-fax number, so the faxes you receive go right into your laptop or BlackBerry. This way, you'll remain in complete control of any faxes, and you'll also be able to respond the second you receive the fax.

Ninety percent of salespeople waste an important opportunity by leaving the reverse side of their business card blank. The only bigger mistake is to fill the reverse side of your business card with information that is absolutely useless to the individuals you are working to influence.

The reverse side of your business card should display one of the following:

- A mission statement
- Mention of awards
- The value a customer receives by doing business with you

Use the reverse of your business card to make a statement that begins to build a perception of you and the results you deliver to those who decide to do business with you. Here is an example of effectively using the reverse side of a business card:

Improving the bottom-line return from your investments in technology through our expertise in lowering total cost of ownership.

If the reverse of your business card had this statement printed on it, a G.U.I.D.O. might pick up your card, take a look, and think, "It would be great if we could improve our return on our technology investments. Let's see what this individual has to offer." This is the reaction you want to create from your business card.

Here is another example of effectively putting the reserve side of an otherwise blank business card to work in the world of counter-intuitive selling:

Winner of the Industry's "Most Innovative New Product Award" for five consecutive years.

Put our innovation to work to win more market share for you!

This statement builds your credibility—by mentioning the awards—and then talks about growing market share. This might also pique a G.U.I.D.O.'s interest.

Before you send your next PowerNote to G.U.I.D.O., make sure you have created your new business card so you can slip it into the envelope. It's time to enter the "No Title World" that you create!

The Successful Seven: Chapter 35
Action Steps for Mastering the Art of Counter-Intuitive Selling

1. Begin to change how you are perceived in the marketplace by **removing your title** from your business card and from your mindset.

2. If you must continue to use a title, remove the world *sales* or anything related to sales from your title.

3. Immediately create your personal counter-intuitive business card and **destroy** your old business cards.

4. Keep the front of your counter-intuitive business card **clean and clutter free**. List only your name, your company name, your mobile phone number, and your e-mail address.

5. If you feel compelled to list a fax number, use an **e-fax number**.

6. Use the **reverse side** of your counter-intuitive business card to share a statement about what you deliver to the marketplace.

7. Get your counter-intuitive business cards **printed today**, and do not send another PowerNote out until you do!

chapter thirty-six

Getting Well-Respected Individuals to Do the Talking for You

By expanding your circle of influence you begin to create top-of-mind awareness. Leverage it into a powerful counter-intuitive selling advantage.

You've just learned that you can change the way your high-priority target prospects and customers perceive you by removing your title—or at least any mention of "sales"—from your business card. Another effective technique for changing both your real and perceived professional status and value is including more than sales activities within your world of counter-intuitive selling.

Making the Most of Community Involvement

Ken's efforts in this area were beginning to pay off in ways that he had never imagined. His confidence was up, he was enjoying his career more, and—most significantly—he was learning more through his growing involvement in the community. His community involvement was also giving Ken a great feeling. *He was giving back to the community that had created his success.*

This year, he decided to step up his involvement by taking on the role of chairman of the United Way's silent auction. His work with the event coordinator had paid off handsomely. He had been so helpful to her in the weeks leading up to the event that during their last meeting, she turned to Ken and said, "By the way, I meant to ask you, is there anyone in particular that you would prefer to have sitting at your table with you? Would you like to look over the guest list before I finalize the seating arrangements?"

As he walked into the ballroom early to make sure that everything was set for the events later that evening, he smiled as he glanced at the namecards on his table. Among the names, he found two G.U.I.D.O.s (Dennis and Kimberly) and two H.E.R.B.s (Charlie and Joanne). One G.U.I.D.O. was a longtime loyal customer, while the other G.U.I.D.O. and the H.E.R.B.s were either prospects or—other than by name—unknown to Ken.

In his mind, Ken could already hear the introductions that would take place later that evening. "Good evening, and welcome to the auction, and thank you so much for supporting the event. By the way, Dennis, have you met Kim? Dennis and I work together on a number of projects; but Kim, I don't believe we've met before. It's great to finally have the pleasure of meeting you."

Ken was relieved that he had urgently taken care of creating his counter-intuitive business cards. The last thing he wanted to have take place tonight would be placing his business card into the hands of one of the guests at his table, only for that guest to look at his card and think, "Oh, this guy's a sales rep!" Perception is important, so Ken was pleased that he leveled the playing field by removing this barrier.

The Counter-Intuitive PowerLunch

Later in the evening, one of the opportunities that Ken was looking for presented itself. As the two G.U.I.D.O.s were talking business, Kim asked Dennis, "What are you working on with Ken? He mentioned during our introductions that the two of you are working on some projects together."

Without even saying a word, Ken was getting the best introduction to Kim that he could ever ask for—*and Dennis was doing it for him!* This made Ken think back to one of the most successful counter-intuitive tools that he was now using to gain new business. Ken now refers to this tool as his counter-intuitive PowerLunch. It works like this:

- Ken identifies a H.E.R.B. or G.U.I.D.O. within a high-potential target prospect who he has met informally through his community involvement, but has not yet interacted with in a business setting.
- Ken contacts this H.E.R.B. or G.U.I.D.O. and says, "I realize we only met briefly, but it got me thinking that you would benefit greatly from meeting one of my customers, Joe Jackson. If nothing else, I believe you'll walk away thinking to yourself 'I'm really glad I took the time to meet Joe. There are some real potential synergies here.' I've mentioned the idea of the meeting to Joe, and he is looking forward to it."
- Ken arranges the lunch and briefs his prize H.E.R.B. or G.U.I.D.O. about the individual with whom they are having lunch, especially as it pertains to the perception and impression that Ken wants his prospect to gain.

Ken has several key customers that he uses for his PowerLunches, and he always returns the favor by making sure that these customers are well taken care of. As a matter of fact, Ken's entire team constantly bends over backward for these special customers, in recognition of the value they bring in creating new business for Ken. In the end, it is a truly win-win situation for both Ken and Ken's customer.

The best aspect of this counter-intuitive tool is what takes place during the PowerLunch. After Ken handles introductions, Ken's guest looks at Ken's customer and says, "Tell me how you know Ken?"

At this point in the PowerLunch, Ken knows he will not be saying *another word*. He relaxes, sits back, and listens as his prized customer tells his high-potential prospect every reason why he needs to be doing business with Ken.

The beauty of the PowerLunch is that, whereas Ken gets paid to say good things about the results he produces for his customers, Ken's customer doesn't get paid to say these things. So when the prospect hears it from Ken's customer, the message is much more powerful than if it had come from Ken.

Getting Involved

As a counter-intuitive selling professional, there are many ways for you to expand your circle of influence. You can do it though community involvement (as Ken did through United Way), professional involvement (through associations within your profession), economic development involvement (through your local chamber of commerce), and educational involvement (by working with the schools and colleges within your community), to name just a few examples.

Here are some other ideas for getting involved that will provide significant benefit to both you and the organization that receives your commitment of time and energy:

- Lead a fund-raising effort for a community organization.
- Head the membership development committee for the chamber of commerce.
- Take a committee chair position with an industry association.
- Offer to assist United Way in targeting the companies in the community that are not yet supporting the effort with internal employee fund drives.
- Offer to help launch a foundation for a newly identified urgent need in the community.
- Donate your time to assist with career development programs within the local schools.
- If there is not one in your area, initiate efforts to form a Sales and Marketing Association within your community.
- Join the board of one of the well-respected charitable/support/development organizations in your community (Salvation Army, Girls Club/Boys Club, etc.).

- Join a community service organization—Rotary Club or Lion's Club, for example—and be actively involved in its efforts.

As a committed counter-intuitive selling professional, it is critical that you realize the importance of believing in any effort that you join. If you do not believe in what you are supporting, you will not be effective, and others will see through your lack of commitment. And remember, every involvement requires a commitment of time and energy, so don't overextend yourself.

Find an organization or effort to which you will commit, get actively involved, and keep the commitments that you make. Your reputation depends on your follow-through. Once you make the commitment and follow through on it, the benefits will be significant—both to you and to the organization that is fortunate enough to gain your involvement.

If you need some advice on where and how to get involved, talk to a G.U.I.D.O. You'll soon discover that almost every G.U.I.D.O. is involved in the community in some way, somewhere—and he or she will probably appreciate your assistance with his or her efforts!

Remember, Ken's introduction to the G.U.I.D.O. that became his newest prospect only happened because Ken was **involved!**

The Successful Seven: Chapter 36
Action Steps for Mastering the Art of Counter-Intuitive Selling

1. Increase your **circle of influence** by expanding your activities to include more than sales activities.

2. Get **involved in the community** by joining organizations with a mission in which you believe and where you know you can make an impact in their results.

3. Use the counter-intuitive PowerLunch to **cross-pollinate** target G.U.I.D.O.s and H.E.R.B.s you meet in your community work with the G.U.I.D.O.s and H.E.R.B.s that do business with you.

4. During a PowerLunch, **let your guests do the talking for you**. Sit back, relax, and enjoy lunch!

5. Be sure that you **do not overextend** your involvement. Pick one organization, get involved, and make an impact.

6. For high visibility, consider undertaking **more challenging involvement opportunities**—the *ones others are afraid to touch*. Your impact will be appreciated.

7. If you need advice on where and how to get involved, **ask a G.U.I.D.O.!**

chapter thirty-seven

Patience Has Its Place in the Counter-Intuitive World

Remember, this is a journey, not a destination.

A major success factor for counter-intuitive selling professionals is learning the **balance between patience and impatience**—both with **ourselves** and with our **high-potential prospects and customers**.

Maintaining a Balance with Yourself and Others

Let's first look at what it means to maintain a balance between patience and impatience with ourselves.

One of my first mentors (the first one from whom I *actually* learned something and improved my results!) put it this way, regarding his role as my sales manager:

> "The balance is where it should be when, as your sales manager, I have patience with your progress and results because I see that you are doing everything you possibly can to build your business and close deals. You are impatient with yourself because, in spite of the fact that you are doing everything that you possibly can to build your business and close deals, you are continually trying to find ways to do more and close more business.
>
> The moment I become impatient, and you become patient, we have a problem."

A key success factor for the counter-intuitive selling professional is to always maintain this balance, both with yourself and with the individual for whom you are producing the results. The counter-intuitive selling professional is always looking for ways to add more genuine opportunities into his or her sales pipeline.

In the end, the true counter-intuitive selling professional is judged on one key factor: **your ability to create business that did not exist before you entered the picture.**

What do I mean by this?

It is the **difference between an order-taker and the counter-intuitive selling professional**. Anyone can take an order, and anyone can fill a need when a G.U.I.D.O. realizes the solution exists. The true counter-intuitive selling professional finds G.U.I.D.O., uncovers his or her issues—*the things that keep G.U.I.D.O. from sleeping at night*—and finds ways to solve these issues. These solutions involve ideas that G.U.I.D.O. was not thinking about before the counter-intuitive selling professional arrived on the scene.

This is why it is essential that you understand whom G.U.I.D.O. really is, and that you do not mistake a N.E.R.D. for a G.U.I.D.O.

Once you identify a G.U.I.D.O. and surround yourself with H.A.N.K.s and H.E.R.B.s, you begin to really understand the issues that G.U.I.D.O. is facing—the ones that are critical to his success and the success of his organization. With that understanding, you can create business that did not exist before you entered the picture. You also can begin to use all of your counter-intuitive selling tools, including PowerNotes, to create the road map to G.U.I.D.O. and his business (review Chapter 32 if you need a reminder about how to use PowerNotes to gain top-of-mind awareness and visibility with G.U.I.D.O.).

Be Careful—and Patient—with G.U.I.D.O!

This is also where practicing patience with your target high-potential prospects and customers comes into play. G.U.I.D.O. does not view you as a salesperson; he views you as a colleague (remember, you have established equal footing with G.U.I.D.O.). He looks to you for advice and guidance, not high-pressure sales tactics.

The minute G.U.I.D.O. senses any high-pressure sales tactics, he is likely to send you into the misery of N.E.R.D.'s world. He will no longer view you as a colleague and advisor. To him you will become "just another sales guy." He'll think to himself, "This is a perfect one to send over to my N.E.R.D. I don't have time to deal with this."

The way to effectively accomplish your goal of doing business with G.U.I.D.O., while making sure that he does not feel pressured in any way, is to **pay *close* attention to G.U.I.D.O.'s signals**. G.U.I.D.O. has his own timeline, which you can influence, especially when you have accurately identified and attached yourself to his most urgent priorities.

If a problem keeps G.U.I.D.O. up at night, you can rest assured that he is looking to solve it quickly. At the point that you make contact with him, he may not have found the solution that he trusts to get the job done. *This is what you bring to the table.*

Your goal, as the counter-intuitive selling professional, is to create a **dissatisfaction gap** in G.U.I.D.O.'s mind. This dissatisfaction gap is best defined as:

> **the gap between the unsatisfactory solution that G.U.I.D.O. is now using (this could be no solution at all) and the solution that you provide.**

With every contact that you initiate with G.U.I.D.O., your goal is to widen the dissatisfaction gap—the gap between your solution and any other possible solution. Without directly stating the obvious, your goal is to get G.U.I.D.O. thinking, "If this is possibly a better solution, we need to look at it."

As your contacts with G.U.I.D.O. begin to feed him more concrete evidence and information regarding what you bring to the table, G.U.I.D.O. begins to think a little deeper about the issues he is trying to solve. He thinks, "If this solution is providing these results to other organizations, we need to take a look at this. What we are using today certainly is not giving us these results."

At some point in your counter-intuitive selling journey with G.U.I.D.O., he will say to himself, "I've seen enough to take a close look at this. This is working for other people; the research proves it. This is proven, and therefore, low risk."

At this turning point in your quest to win G.U.I.D.O.'s top-of-mind awareness and visibility, you have achieved success. You have answered the five burning questions in G.U.I.D.O.'s mind:

1. Does this solution address one of my pressing issues?
2. Does it really deliver results?
3. Where is the evidence?
4. Who else says this solution works?
5. Is this a low-risk solution, compared to other alternatives?

When you have answered these questions for G.U.I.D.O. through all of your contact—both direct and indirect—you have won the battle of counter-intuitive selling. Your success might have been the result of some combination of your calls, your counter-intuitive letter campaign, your PowerNotes, your community involvement, and PowerLunches. Somewhere along the way, G.U.I.D.O. made his own decision, in his own mind, **on his own timetable**, and said to himself, "I'm ready to look at this, and I *need* to look at this."

The key factor for success on your end was that you patiently allowed G.U.I.D.O. to "**reach out from the inside**" on *his timetable*—not yours. Your role involved doing everything you possibly could to accelerate his decision-making process, without "**pounding from the outside**" too hard.

The Successful Seven: Chapter 37
Action Steps for Mastering the Art of Counter-Intuitive Selling

1. Be sure to sustain the correct **balance between patience and impatience** when it comes to your relationship with the individual for whom you produce results. *You need to be impatient while your manager remains patient.*

2. Remember that, as a counter-intuitive selling professional, you are ultimately judged on one key factor: **your ability to create business that did not exist before you entered the picture.** Make sure you are "creating" new business on a daily basis.

3. Realize that G.U.I.D.O. has **his own timetable** and that he will not be "pressured" into working on your timetable. Be patient with G.U.I.D.O. when it will work in your favor.

4. Do not attempt to pressure G.U.I.D.O. unless you want to visit N.E.R.D.'s world.

5. Create the **dissatisfaction gap** in G.U.I.D.O.'s mind between your solution and all other solutions. Doing this will create a sense of urgency in G.U.I.D.O.'s mind.

6. Use all of the counter-intuitive selling tools at your disposal to answer the **five burning questions** in G.U.I.D.O.'s mind.

7. Work to accelerate G.U.I.D.O.'s decision-making process, but have the patience to allow him to "**reach from the inside**."

Checks and Balances: Keep Your Currency Rising

Staying in the world of counter-intuitive selling

chapter thirty-eight

Proven Success Accelerators: The Role Mentors Play

Learning from mentors who share the roles of the individuals you need to get to will accelerate your success faster than any other counter-intuitive selling tool.

Selling can be a lonely game. In many ways it is an individual contributor sport. Even with all of the talk today about team selling and "the team bringing home the big deal," in many situations it still boils down to one thing: the sales pro out there in front of prospects, working solo to find what could be the next big deal.

Especially with the technology at the fingertips of today's salesperson, he or she can easily spend a large portion of time communicating with, but not really in touch with, real people.

So how does the counter-intuitive selling professional stay connected?

The key lies in your **network of mentors**—not just a single mentor.

The Mentor Mix

It is critical to remember that a mentoring relationship is a two-way street. There needs to be value in the relationship for both of you. Otherwise, the relationship will not last, and it will not evolve. Mentors will keep you current in many ways, and different mentors fill the different needs that you have as a business and sales professional. At the same time, you also fill different needs for each of your mentors.

Frank, the mentor you've read about in this book, is actually a composite of four mentors in my life. Each one has played a different role, and each one occupied a different level of relevance and importance in my life over the past 20+ years. I recently traveled across the globe to reconnect with one of these mentors. The relationship is that important to both of us!

Let's talk about why it is important to have a mix of mentors in your career.

As you enter the world of counter-intuitive selling, it is critical that you gain a well-rounded view of the world of business. There is no place better from which to gain this perspective than through a network of mentors. Establishing a mentoring relationship with a G.U.I.D.O. that you meet through your community involvement is another way to learn more about the world of G.U.I.D.O.s and to be in touch with the issues that G.U.I.D.O.s face on a daily basis.

This does not mean, however, that all of your mentors should be G.U.I.D.O.s. Establishing mentoring relationships at different levels within the business community will enable you to share the perspective of many of the individuals that you will deal with in the world of counter-intuitive selling—*while accelerating your journey and your results.*

It's vital that you establish mentoring relationships within all areas of business. You need to understand the mindset of all of the functional areas that make up a typical business. Most salespeople gravitate toward mentors that come from the sales world. While this will certainly improve your skills as a salesperson, it may not provide a full view of how decisions are made and how the business world operates—a view that you need in order to be successful in counter-intuitive selling.

As you begin to build out your mentor network, look for individuals with roles in these professional areas:

- *CEO/president.* Mentoring with a top-notch/top-level G.U.I.D.O. has the potential to significantly accelerate your understanding of the world of counter-intuitive selling.

- *Sales/marketing.* Many sales professionals gravitate to establish a mentoring relationship with others in sales and marketing, and it's vitally important to have a mentor in this field.
- *Financial.* Understanding how the world of finance operates within both public and private companies is essential to your success. Make sure you mentor with a top level financial expert, preferably a CFO.
- *Operations.* Leading the actual operations of any large company requires a unique set of skills, and rest assured that when it comes to any significant purchase by the company, the head of operations definitely has a say in the decision. You will learn a lot from a mentor with operations expertise.
- *Administration/HR.* The back office and people side of any business deals with its own unique set of priorities and challenges, and it's important that you know how these leaders think and make decisions.

Just Ask

Perhaps you are sitting there right now thinking to yourself, "This is not going to be easy! How do I approach these senior people and ask them to consider being my mentor?"

The answer may be simpler than you think (remember, we make things more complicated than they really are): **just ask!**

Although you may be thinking that most accomplished business executives will be hard to approach, you will find that most of them will be honored by your request for mentoring. It will be important to be prepared to share with the individual why you decided to seek him or her out specifically, and what you would like to gain from the relationship.

In return, be sure to ask prospective mentors what they expect from you in the relationship, and how you can help them. Then, make sure you can deliver on their expectations before you make a commitment to enter the mentoring relationship. If they don't initially have any expectations of you within the mentoring relationship, ask them to give it some thought and to let you know the next time you meet. A one-way mentoring relationship is not destined for a long life!

It is also critical to make sure that you only establish as many mentoring relationships as you realistically will be able to handle. Start with one solid mentor, establish the relationship, and then decide if you have the time available for another one. Always firmly establish any mentoring relationship over a period of several months before you add an additional mentor.

As your group of mentors grows, look to include H.A.N.K.s and H.E.R.B.s in the mix. These highly valued individuals play a significant role in your success as a counter-intuitive selling professional, so mentoring with them will grow your understanding of and ability to relate to them.

As a counter-intuitive selling professional, you should always be thinking outside the box, so look to also include—at some point in the not-too-distant future—a N.E.R.D. as a mentor. Once you mentor with a N.E.R.D., you may say to yourself, "I don't agree with the *way* this N.E.R.D. thinks, but I understand <u>how</u> he thinks." That understanding is critical to your career!

Selecting Your Mentors

A final thought on mentors. Many counter-intuitive selling professionals ask, "Should I pick my customers as mentors? Should I pick my target high-potential prospects as mentors? Who should I select?"

Select your potential mentors based on the value they will add to your career, rather than on their status as a customer or prospect. Keep your mentor selection focused on the type of individual you are seeking to gain knowledge from—not anything else. The most important mentor in my life never actually did any business with me directly, but he directed me to more business than I could ever count.

Treat your mentor relationships with a high level of respect, and get to know your mentor's executive assistant very well. Learn everything you can from the assistant about your mentor. You will gain an added perspective that will prove invaluable to you.

There is another extremely valuable experience you'll gain from your mentors. You'll have the opportunity to learn from them what it is like to be a mentor, and this is something that you will need as you become extremely successful in the world of counter-intuitive selling. You see, as your success grows, it won't be long until someone asks you to be a mentor.

Don't worry, though. As a well-trained counter-intuitive selling expert, you'll be well prepared for the challenge.

The Successful Seven: Chapter 38
Action Steps for Mastering the Art of Counter-Intuitive Selling

1. Build your mentor network **one solid mentoring relationship** at a time.

2. Remember that a mentoring relationship is a **two-way street**. Be sure you understand and deliver on what your mentor expects from you.

3. Establish mentoring relationships in **all functional areas** of the typical company to *gain the perspective you need to be successful in the world of counter-intuitive selling.*

4. **Don't limit your mentors** to include only G.U.I.D.O.s—*include H.A.N.K.s, H.E.R.B.s, and, yes, even a N.E.R.D.* (for a period of time!).

5. **Look beyond your customers and prospects** for potential mentors.

6. Get to know **your mentor's executive assistant** as well as you know your mentor.

7. **Learn the art of mentoring** from your best mentors so that you are prepared when it's your turn!

chapter thirty-nine

Working Through Your
Ongoing Challenges

Throughout your journey into the world of counter-intuitive selling you will be challenged. Sticking to the basics will help you solve your challenges.

Entering the world of counter-intuitive selling is a long journey—one that can bring great rewards. During this journey, however, it will be quite easy for you to make a wrong turn and head down the wrong path. You may find yourself struggling, and not even realize it at first.

In order to discover just how you can go off-track, we need to return to the very beginning of your journey into the world of counter-intuitive selling. What I shared in the beginning of the book is worth revisiting as you begin to put more and more of your counter-intuitive selling tools to work to dramatically alter your career.

Embracing and Working Toward Change

If you are going to change your results—your sales results—you are going to need to change what you do today. Remember our definition of insanity from Chapter 1: **doing the same things we've always done and expecting different results.**

For your journey into the world of counter-intuitive selling to be successful and for your selling results to change, **you must be open to change.** You need to develop **the mindset that change is good.** Otherwise, no matter what you do to develop your counter-intuitive selling skills, nothing will change. (Does that sound like something close to insanity?)

Although this is the first step, it is not the only step. Just thinking about change and saying, "I need to do things differently from now on," is *not* going to change anything.

Remember, *it takes at least 21 days to change an old habit and replace it with a new, more effective habit.* That means **21 consecutive days** of doing something a different way before the habit becomes a learned habit—one you don't need to think about before automatically responding in the new way.

If you do something consistently for 14 or 15 days, and then you realize that you slip up and go back to your old habit, you need to restart your 21-day period of consistent, continual practice **from the beginning**!

Only after 21 consecutive days of continual practice can a "new or different" way of doing things become a learned habit. At that point, you will act differently without needing to remind yourself, "I need to do this differently, just like I've been practicing."

Feeling Uncomfortable While Learning New Skills

Although as human beings, we do not like to feel uncomfortable, that feeling is a very positive sign during your journey into the world of counter-intuitive selling. Feeling uncomfortable usually means that you are in an unfamiliar environment (such as G.U.I.D.O.'s office), you are saying something in a new and different way (calling and talking to G.U.I.D.O. without starting the call by telling him who you are), or you are doing something that you have not done in the past on a regular basis (getting involved to chair a committee or an event).

In reality, each time you do something, you begin to feel more comfortable in doing it. Knowing that new things will feel uncomfortable—**and that this is a positive sign**—will help to keep you on-track with your commitments to change as you enter the world of counter-intuitive selling.

Remembering to Use *Time-Spaced Repetition*

How many times have you gone to a one-day seminar? At the seminar you probably heard a lot of good ideas. If it was a particularly effective seminar, you probably even conducted a short role-play, so you could actually "practice" what you were "learning."

A month or so after the one-day seminar, you see the workbook from the event sitting on the corner of your desk, and you think to yourself, "I'd forgotten about that seminar. There were a lot of great ideas shared that day, but I can't seem to remember any of them."

There is a very good explanation for why you are not acting on anything that you experienced in the seminar: There was no **time-spaced repetition practice**, which is necessary for any behavioral change to take hold—to form new and better habits.

Remember, great ideas do not change behavior.

Making and Keeping I-Team Appointments

Your I-Team appointments with yourself are the time you use to change habits by working on your time-spaced repetition. Your I-Team appointments need to be a permanent element of your calendar; these should not change for anyone, not even G.U.I.D.O!

If you do not perfect your skills though practice, you will never get the opportunity to talk with a G.U.I.D.O. Don't waste the opportunities that you do get when you actually get a G.U.I.D.O. on the phone. Be prepared through regular practice. (If you need a reminder of the important of practice, revisit the Ozzie Smith story in Chapter 2.)

Ideally, space your I-Team appointments out each week, making sure that you have at least one hour scheduled every other day, as close to the same time each day as possible. For example, schedule 3 PM to 4 PM every day or at least every Monday, Wednesday, and Friday. Treat your I-Team appointments the same way you treat an appointment with a G.U.I.D.O. at your number one customer or high-potential target prospect. There are very few "emergencies" that arise that should force you to change the appointment. Your I-Team time is *critical* to your career!

Using Behavioral Change Triggers

Make a behavioral trigger with the following message to remind you of the importance of using triggers:

> **use triggers →change behavior**

As human beings, we are creatures of habit, regardless of whether the habits are good or bad. Unless we use something—**a trigger**—to force our habits to change, we will never effectively create behavioral change. The most successful counter-intuitive selling professionals use behavioral triggers on a regular basis—and never stop using this highly effective tool.

Make a commitment that during one of your weekly I-Team appointments you will set ten minutes aside to create one to three new behavioral triggers. If some of your desired habits are still "a work in progress," continue to use one of your existing behavioral triggers to refine your new habits. Commit to instituting at least one new behavioral trigger every week.

Remember:

You are the CEO of your success.

Your future success is in your hands. Use your counter-intuitive behavior changing tools wisely!

The Successful Seven: Chapter 39
Action Steps for Mastering the Art of Counter-Intuitive Selling

1. In order to successfully enter the world of counter-intuitive selling you are going to need to **drastically change** the things you do on a daily basis.

2. Develop the mindset that **change is good.**

3. For a desired new behavior to become a learned habit, it must be practiced for at least **21 <u>consecutive</u> days**.

4. Strive to **feel uncomfortable** as you enter the world of counter-intuitive selling. Feeling uncomfortable means that you are growing and changing old habits. Learn to accept that feeling uncomfortable is good.

5. Incorporate **time-spaced repetition** practice into your daily and weekly **I-Team appointments.**

6. Treat your daily and weekly I-Team appointments just as you would an appointment with your number one target G.U.I.D.O. **Don't let anything get in the way** of keeping these on your calendar!

7. Utilize **behavioral change triggers** to force the development of new habits. Create at least **one new behavioral trigger each week**.

Appendix

Continue Your Counter-Intuitive Selling Journey at
www.counter-intuitiveselling.com

Bill Byron Concevitch practices counter-intuitive selling everyday—in the field selling and coaching sales professionals around the globe. Like you, these sales pros want to continue to learn from the creator of counter-intuitive selling.

www.counter-intuitiveselling.com is your direct connection to everything counter-intuitive, including:

- Daily updates from the **real world** of counter-intuitive selling
- More great articles and publications from the author
- Sales tools for the counter-intuitive selling professional
- Direct connection to a **sales coach online**, where you can ask the expert and get professional advice on your specific selling challenges
- Success stories from other counter-intuitive selling professionals
- Information on where you can experience counter-intuitive selling **live**
- **Sneak previews** of new counter-intuitive material, before it is released to the general population of sales professionals
- Information on corporate sales training programs, designed to enable entire sales forces and sales management teams to benefit from the application of counter-intuitive selling

Log on today at *www.counter-intuitiveselling.com.*
You can also reach Bill Byron Concevitch at *bbc@counter-intuitiveselling.com.*

About the Author

Named one of the top 20 people to watch as "movers, shakers, and thought leaders" by *Lifelong Learning Market Report,* Bill Byron Concevitch has an unparalleled track record in today's challenging business environment.

Bill works with organizations large and small, from Fortune 500 companies to start-up organizations. His specialty is working with teams of sales professionals to identify and develop the skills needed to exceed their own performance objectives. The trademarks of Bill's programs that lead to success for the participants are *easy-to-execute gameplans and documented results.*

As chief talent and learning officer for Witness Systems (NASDAQ:WITS), Bill leads all of the people, talent, and learning initiatives for employees, partners, and customers for the global leader in workforce optimization. As the former senior vice president of Element K (formerly Ziff-Davis Education) and chief learning officer of ExecuTrain Corporation, Bill understands the talent and learning industries from a very unique perspective. Bill has also served as president of Mentergy, executive vice president of KnowledgePool (the Fujitsu eLearning Company), and executive vice president of Learning Tree International.

During his tenure at ExecuTrain Corporation, Bill led the efforts in product development, emerging technologies, training/certification, and research and development. He was responsible for the design and launch of the ExecuTrain Virtual University® and the adoption of High-Performance Learning™ as a revolutionary approach to integrating technology into classroom education and training.

Bill's career in the training and education field began with the Dale Carnegie® Organization, where he assisted his institute in achieving the President's Cup Award, a recognition that less than 10 percent of the institutes around the world accomplish. He has also held senior-level positions within the staffing and recruiting industry.

Bill's career began as a salesperson, regional supervisor, and vice president of training and development for a major specialty retailer. Under his direction, the company was awarded the coveted "Retailer of the Year" award in its industry segment—for its **counter-intuitive approach** to selling. His sales and management experience continued as a salesperson and later sales director for major Fortune 500 corporations, and as senior vice president of an international van line agency.

Bill is featured in industry forums and events, and has appeared on "Breakfast with Dell" and "Business Across America." Bill serves as a judge of the annual *Brandon Hall Excellence in eLearning Awards*. He also teaches public speaking at the collegiate level.

Bill is the author of *Increasing the Odds: Sales Is Not A Numbers Game* and the soon-to-be published *Turning Learning Inside Out: The Learner-Driven Approach to Peak Performance*. He is regularly quoted in IT, training, education, and sales publications, and is the author of numerous white papers on trends in workplace learning, talent technology, and business.

Index